CUT THE CRAP

AND FEEL AMAZING

HYPNOTHERAPY DOWNLOADS
BY AILSA FRANK

Take Control of Alcohol

Stop Binge Drinking for Women

Stop Binge Drinking for Men

Build Confidence & Self-esteem

Money – Increase Your Wealth

Get Out of Debt

Weight Loss for Women

Weight Loss for Men

Heartbreak and Loss

Comfortable Sex for Women

Let Go of Health Worries

De-stress Your Life

Stop Worrying

Study Motivation and Exam Success

Relaxation for Children and Teens

Visit www.ailsafrank.com to check for new titles.

CUT
THE CRAP

✂ -

AND FEEL
AMAZING

AILSA FRANK

HAY HOUSE

Carlsbad, California • New York City
London • Sydney • New Delhi

Published in the United Kingdom by:
Hay House UK Ltd, The Sixth Floor, Watson House,
54 Baker Street, London W1U 7BU
Tel: +44 (0)20 3927 7290; Fax: +44 (0)20 3927 7291
www.hayhouse.co.uk

Published in the United States of America by:
Hay House Inc., PO Box 5100, Carlsbad, CA 92018-5100
Tel: (1) 760 431 7695 or (800) 654 5126
Fax: (1) 760 431 6948 or (800) 650 5115
www.hayhouse.com

Published in Australia by:
Hay House Australia Ltd, 18/36 Ralph St, Alexandria NSW 2015
Tel: (61) 2 9669 4299; Fax: (61) 2 9669 4144
www.hayhouse.com.au

A catalogue record for this book is available from the British Library.

ISBN: 978-1-4019-6842-7

Layout by Matt Swann Creative Ltd.

For Assaf, Francesca, Jane, Lydia, Dana, my AMAZING clients, the staff at Starbucks in Camberley for making me coffees during the writing of this book and everyone who has been part of my life.

CONTENTS

INTRODUCTION

Every action in life has a consequence, which might be brief and contained or, like the ripple created when you drop a pebble into a lake, it may spread out. Sometimes, situations arise in our lives as the result of our own actions and reactions, and sometimes other people's actions send out the ripples that create our reality.

As children, we have little, if any, control over the circumstances of our own lives. And although we have more control as adults, the choices and decisions we make will be based on our upbringing and childhood experiences. But whatever those experiences have been, each one of us ultimately has the ability to steer our own life course.

I was able to write this book because of my life experiences, because of the questions I have asked, the answers I have discovered, and the years I have spent working as a therapist, helping people to improve their mindset and cope better with their own lives.

Life is simply a series of phases, each one leading you on to the next, which is something worth remembering if you're experiencing stressful or challenging times: whatever is happening is a phase and you will pass through it.

In 2002, my life looked perfect – from the outside. Behind the scenes, however, my 19-year marriage was falling apart. And so was I. In the autumn of that year, I had a mental breakdown and spent a period of time in a psychiatric unit, which is when my whole world changed. My life flipped dramatically from working and being a mother to my gorgeous 10-year-old daughter to later living alone in a bedsit.

I had been a kind and caring person, but in the process of always looking out for others I had ignored my own needs for too long, until eventually I'd become so swamped by everyone else's cares and responsibilities that I lost myself. Then, after my marriage broke down, the people I assumed would be there for me, weren't. I know for some of them it was because they were scared by my behaviour during my mental breakdown and didn't know how to react to me.

The bottom line was that as well as losing my mind, I lost custody of my daughter, my home, my family, my friends, my dog, my money, my car and my belongings. It was as if my entire world had been erased like chalk from a blackboard. As a loving and devoted mother, I had spent 10 years trying to make my daughter's world perfect. Then, in one fell swoop, I had let her down. I did eventually rebuild my relationship with her, but it would be eight years before I saw her on her birthday again, and even longer than that before I spent another Christmas day with her. What I missed most during that time was just being there for her and doing all the normal things we take for granted, such as making breakfast and watching television together.

Through the most difficult and lonely times, I struggled to rebuild my life and come to terms with the fact that I couldn't simply step back into the world I'd dropped out of, because my breakdown had changed everything. Instead, I had to search for ways to help myself so that I could be strong, not only for my own sake but also for my daughter. I chose not to take anti-depressants during that time, because I knew that they would simply mask my underlying problems. What I had to do was face my circumstances head on and learn to cope with my new reality.

I made a decision quite early on during the period of my recovery that, somehow, my life would be AMAZING, despite everything that had happened. Today, perhaps the most AMAZING thing about it is the relationship I now have with my daughter.

Luckily, during the lowest point in my life, I met someone who loved and supported me, because he could see who I really was. He told me later that the reason he had stayed with me during some of my low points was because he could see that, even when I was desperate because I had no contact with my child, I was constantly moving forward. That man is now my husband, and the support he gave me at that terrible time helped me enormously. I realized then that the key to improving your life is to keep changing and evolving by changing your mindset, so that you never become stuck in a bad situation.

Although I now have good relationships with my family and ex-husband, I know what it feels like not to be believed or approved of by your friends and family, and how difficult it is to have to learn to cope alone. I also know that if I can change myself and the circumstances of my life, every client who comes to me feeling lost, stressed, upset or unable to cope can make their life AMAZING too.

When I started out as a therapist, I hoped to be able to use the knowledge I had gained for myself to help just one person. Little did I know that I would end up helping thousands, which is something I'm immensely proud of, because everyone's life matters – not just to them, but to me too.

I wrote this book to share with as many people as possible the knowledge and tools I have found to be effective, so that they can avoid or find solutions to their own problems and learn how to Cut the Crap and Feel AMAZING. Many people have more skills and more knowledge based on their own life experiences than they realize. So even when you think you can't achieve something, you probably can. 'Cutting the crap and feeling AMAZING' is all about rising above the negative and the dramas, learning how to manage your life better, and changing whatever needs to be changed to enable you to get into the AMAZING zone. By applying my creative techniques to move your mind into positive thinking, combined with some common sense, you can learn to help yourself.

From the moment you start to read this book you will start to change the way you think. Apply the 'AMAZING' to your life from the outset and watch the process of transformation begin. Read the book, then reread it – or at least the chapters that are most relevant to you. Then incorporate the simple techniques into your daily routine so that they become part of your way of life.

What you are about to read in the following chapters will make your dreams more positive, and then help you to make those dreams come true.

Stop trying to control everything.
Let your life be an adventure.
Cut out the negative and feel AMAZING.

CHAPTER 1

GET INTO THE AMAZING ZONE

Focus on the life you want, not the life you have had

I developed the concept of the AMAZING zone many years ago to help myself when working under high pressure. Later, I applied it to my personal life to help me deal with difficult times and then to help clients through my hypnotherapy work. The AMAZING zone bypasses fears, worries, self-doubt and distress. It is a simple concept that is easy to remember, and it really works. I teach the AMAZING zone to my hypnotherapy clients, many of whom come back later to tell me AMAZING stories about the ways in which their lives have worked out well.

As a hypnotherapist, I know the power of the subconscious mind: every time you talk to yourself you are, in effect, hypnotizing yourself. If what you tell yourself is negative, you will eventually be programmed into believing that negative thought. But if your self-talk is positive, you will program yourself positively. And it isn't only what you say to yourself that will have this effect. You are also being constantly programmed – positively and negatively – by other people, by the situations in which you find yourself and by past experiences that have formed the foundation of your belief system.

What is the AMAZING zone?

Imagine all the crap in your life right now (stress, worries, fears, negative emotions, money problems, work and relationship issues...) and then imagine **rising above it all**, feeling empowered as all the negative issues resolve because you have found everything you need to make them work out well. Feeling stuck simply leads to more feelings of being stuck. By rising above everything, good or bad, saying 'It's AMAZING' and feeling optimistic that things will work out AMAZINGLY well, you will expect nothing less than AMAZING and, over time, this is the result you will achieve.

When you think and talk AMAZING, you will find yourself in the right place at the right time for AMAZING things to happen. Even when everything seems to be going wrong, let the frustration pass and persist in saying 'AMAZING'. It's a bit like the positive person who falls into dog mess and comes up smelling of roses: if you are positive about even a negative event, it will turn out positively.

Being in the AMAZING zone is easy because you only need to remember one thing, which is to think and feel AMAZING. There may be moments when a real crisis is occurring and you forget to feel AMAZING for a few moments. But that's okay, because you'll soon remember to get back into AMAZING thinking again.

Apply the AMAZING to your life right now. Think of all the things you would like to change and start to repeat the word 'AMAZING'.

Many people who try to help themselves end up focusing on the life they *had* instead of on the life they want to have. There are lots of talking therapies that focus on the negative past without providing any tools for dealing with the now. I learned that the best way to detach yourself from your negative problems, injustices of the past and emotional turmoil, is to cut free from them by focusing all your thoughts on the now and on the future life you desire to have. If you hear yourself talking negatively or dwelling on something, say to yourself, 'Just cut the crap and feel AMAZING,' and tap into your AMAZING memory bank.

If you are struggling to feel the AMAZING feeling, it is because your subconscious mind is programmed with negative beliefs. The following technique will help to release them so that you can begin to think more positively.

Pebbles-in-the-pond technique

Imagine that you are in a garden, standing beside a pond with golden-coloured water reflecting the sunlight. Imagine that there are colourful pebbles around the edge of the pond, each one representing something negative that you need to let go of. Imagine throwing the pebbles into the pond. As each one goes in, imagine it dissolving in the colourful water. Let the negative feelings and pebbles disappear. Visualize the pebbles dissolving one by one and feel the relief as you let them go. As you let go of the negative you will make room for positive thoughts in your mind. Think of all the AMAZING things that have happened in your life, such as when you got a job, a bargain in a shop, the keys to your first home, or some good news. Thinking about those things will help to remind you of the good feelings and clear the negative from your mind.

Feel the feeling of being free as you feel AMAZING, for example running on a beach or in a field, spinning on the spot with your arms open wide in front of the Eiffel Tower, mountain biking with the wind blowing in your face, or whatever feels right for you. Feel the feeling of life being exciting, so that you can be open to AMAZING things happening to improve your life.

Good can come out of a bad situation

People's lives can be terrible. Truly awful things can happen, or life can be challenging on a daily basis. I'm not suggesting that you should simply brush those experiences under the carpet and forget about them. It's important to ACCEPT that they happened, UNDERSTAND why they happened, LEARN from them and MOVE ON from them. You can imagine throwing the unwanted thoughts into the pond like pebbles so that you get back into the AMAZING zone as quickly as possible. Practise the AMAZING feelings.

Try to look for the good in any situation. Many people turn a negative experience into a positive life-changing event. Low points are turning points. Sometimes a really bad situation will make you address an issue, or you'll have no choice but to make changes that turn out to be AMAZING. The worst thing is to get caught up in a negative that absorbs you. You need to find an inner strength to get out of it. Demand something better for yourself and be creative to find solutions, using the AMAZING zone feeling to lift you out of where you are into a better place within yourself. Be inspired by people who have done something positive as a result of a negative situation, such as:

- the parent who loses a child and goes on to create an AMAZING charity to help children with cancer

- the recovered drug addict who helps young people build AMAZING lives

- the person who loses their job and goes on to create an AMAZING business employing other people

- the person who loses a loved one and goes on to have an AMAZING life as a tribute to them.

What we focus on, talk about, think about or self-chatter about becomes our reality, because we program ourselves, just like the person who is determined to become a doctor when everyone is telling them they can't do it and proves them all wrong by believing they can, studying hard and making it happen.

Life is pretty simple: the more you focus on the things you want, the more you become those things. If you dwell on the past, you will create more distance between you and your future. If you focus on your future, setting goals and actioning the steps that need to be taken, you will reach that future place more quickly. If you persist in believing in an AMAZING life, that is exactly what you will get.

The simplest way to create positive things in your life is to say, 'It is AMAZING.' Even if what is going on right now is challenging, say 'It is AMAZING. It is working out AMAZINGLY well.'

When you get into the habit of seeing the positive, you will reprogram yourself to think the positive and soon you will be living the positive. It is you who is creating it, not an outside force or other people, as it is your subconscious mind that holds your set of beliefs. It all begins with you, because how you choose to see things and the words you use are, in effect, hypnotizing you.

If two people are going through a similar situation, one of them may get into the negative drama, while the other may say 'It's AMAZING' and, before they know it, the whole situation will have turned around or something positive will come out of it. Sometimes, difficulties teach us our most important lessons in life. See everything as an opportunity to improve. Gradually cut the negativity from your life and feel AMAZING.

Stepping-stone technique

Accepting simply means acknowledging that things may not always have been great and imagining that your past was simply a series of stepping stones in your journey through life. See in your mind all of your past experiences as stepping stones – solid objects that are useful to you as you move from one piece of solid ground to the next. Let any angry emotions of the past dissolve. Everything we experience, whether good or bad, helps to build our character, gives us life experience, helps us to feel a full spectrum of emotions, and gives us more understanding of what we don't want so that we can aspire to what we do want.

Each stone represents valuable learning. Everyone in history has done the best they could with the knowledge they had. Every person you have known has done the best they could do. And you have done the best you could do, too.

Imagine leaving the past in the past as you walk forwards along the stepping-stone path. From now onwards, believe in great things and have the determination to grasp opportunities as they arise so that they will lead you to the life you want. Seeing your past and future experiences as stepping stones will allow you to let go of the emotions of the past and release fears about the future. The key to getting your life back into balance is to start feeling better in yourself so that you create good choices, which in turn will create a harmonious life. Imagine the stepping stones at any time and feel the feeling of being on a path that is solid both behind you, in your past, and ahead of you, in your future.

It might help to read this section again and practise the technique it describes.

So how can I make my life AMAZING?

Start by saying to yourself 'My life is AMAZING.' In the following chapters, you will read about how to shift the negative beliefs in each area in your life. Trying to feel good about something that has not yet happened can be difficult. One way of doing it is to visualize the results you want. Hypnotherapists work with clients to help them see the outcome of what they want. For example, a smoker imagines they are a non-smoker and how they will feel throughout their day without cigarettes. If you imagine something you want to happen has already worked out AMAZINGLY well and you are celebrating a good result after the event, this will make it easier for you to feel the AMAZING feeling more strongly. Racing drivers use these techniques by visualizing going repeatedly around the track before they drive around it. In their mind, they practise the gear changes and the braking points on each corner.

People are often so busy rushing through life that they don't notice the AMAZING things going on around them. When you are aware of a good moment, take a conscious 'snapshot in my mind' of the moment itself, how it feels and the AMAZING feeling. By being aware of the positive moment as it happens in the NOW, you can recall the memory very strongly at any time in the future. Build a memory bank of AMAZING 'snapshot' moments as they happen to strengthen your AMAZING zone.

Having spent years improving people's belief systems through my work as a hypnotherapist, I have found the word 'AMAZING' and the 'AMAZING feeling' really fast-track you to feeling great and living an AMAZING life. 'AMAZING' is a powerful word, which really works to make great things happen. And it is simple – just one technique and one thing to remember.

- Imagine you are working in an AMAZING job.

- Imagine you have returned from an AMAZING holiday.

- Imagine you live in an AMAZING home.

The best way to create AMAZING feelings is to think about people who are having a great life. A useful hypnotherapy technique is to imagine the life of someone who has what you want. By stepping into the life of someone else, you can begin to imagine how it might feel. Think of someone who has the things you would like to have. For some people, that will be a happy marriage. For others, it will be financial security, or a great job, or a relaxed and happy life. WE ARE ALL DIFFERENT AND WE ALL ENJOY DIFFERENT THINGS. So think about someone who has some of the elements in their life that would make your life enjoyable. Imagine how it would feel to have the security, the love, the happiness, the choices that the person you are thinking about has. Also, think of times when AMAZING things happened to you – for example when you met someone unexpectedly or caught a bus or a train against all odds. We have all had moments in our lives when things have worked out well. Feel the satisfaction and relief that you feel when things go well. Start today to remember more and more good things that have happened to you already. This will help you to program yourself positively to develop your AMAZING ZONE.

From now on, assume that everything is AMAZING FOR YOU. Everyone has experienced something not happening or not working out initially, and then something better coming along – for example not getting a job that you truly believed to be right for you and then better work coming your way, or falling in love with a property you didn't get and then getting something even better suited to you. You can't always see the whole picture, but when it is revealed, you wonder why you worried so much. In other words, start trusting that AMAZING things are happening and everything is working out well for you. An example of this would be somebody getting an illness. It seems that the end of the world has come. But then the illness makes them reassess their life, change their stress levels, start eating properly and looking after themselves, and value the people close to them. In fact, the illness turns out to be a wake-up call that prompts the person to change their life into something very positive.

Imagine you are celebrating AMAZING things happening in your life. Automatically feel the celebration feeling of things working out as well as they can. Say to yourself, 'Yes, it worked out AMAZINGLY well.'

Feeling the AMAZING feeling is not an excuse to avoid getting things done. You still need to be getting on with your life and making decisions. But you are creating inner calm because you know that it will all work out fine.

Program yourself with solutions to change your life so that you can feel better.

If your life is too busy, you will feel that you have no time to yourself. If you make time for yourself, you will be happier.

If your life is empty, you will feel alone. If you find interesting things to fill your life with, your life will become more satisfying.

If your life is financially overstretched, you will feel that you don't have enough money. If you cut back on your spending, you will become happier about your finances.

However, if you allow yourself to feel AMAZING, your life will become truly AMAZING.

In Chapter 3 you will learn how to let go of blockages that may be stopping you from feeling AMAZING feelings. If you suffer from depression or low feelings, take extra time to absorb the information in Chapter 3.

By changing your feelings to AMAZING feelings, you will feel different about your life, then positive things will begin to happen and you will be more solution-focused.

AMAZING day technique

I teach clients to SMILE at bedtime before they go to sleep and to imagine tomorrow has turned out to be AMAZING. Also imagine a positive film in your mind of you being happy during the day. When you get up the next morning, you will feel more positive, which will help to create the AMAZING day you have already programmed to happen. If you imagine things are AMAZING, you will get more done, you will make better choices in your day and you will be more relaxed.

Think of your newfound AMAZING feelings as being the result of MARY POPPINS dropping into your life to sort everything out. She magically made impossible things happen. Your AMAZING feelings will do the same. The AMAZING will dissolve the bad feelings. This will give you the head space and clarity of mind to get on with sorting out the things you need to sort out.

Here is an example of how I used the AMAZING feelings to make an AMAZING day happen for me. Back in 2003, my new partner who later became my second husband booked a photography course in Bradford. When he told me about it, my immediate thought was 'Why Bradford?' which is nearly 4 hours' drive from where we were living at the time. We lived just an hour from London, where there are many photography courses on offer. But instead of asking the question, I immediately reminded myself to feel the AMAZING feeling that it would be great for us.

We travelled up to Bradford the day before the course started and booked into a hotel. At 9 o'clock the next morning, I dropped my partner at the course and then set off to drive through the city. I had no map or satnav, and no Internet on my phone. I felt the feeling of having an AMAZING day and knew that I would be back in time to pick him up at 5 p.m. Then I literally followed my instincts, turning left at one road junction, going straight ahead at another, but always with the feeling of it being AMAZING.

I drove through Bradford city centre and then out into the countryside. Eventually, I pulled up at a huge renovated brick factory building that had been turned into an art gallery housing one of the biggest collections of the works of the British artist David Hockney. I was smiling to myself, because a few weeks earlier in an art class I was attending, the teacher had commented that my style reminded her of David Hockney and that it might be of benefit to me to do some research into his work. I had seen one of his portraits at a London gallery and had wondered at the time where I could find a large collection of his work. But I had said to myself 'AMAZING, I will find his work. It will all work out well.' Now I found myself looking at one of the best collections of his art in the world.

This is the power of the AMAZING feeling – never making anything a drama or believing that something will be hard to achieve, but instead flowing, trusting and feeling AMAZING.

Having had a great day out enjoying the paintings and the little shops and cafés in the village of Saltaire, I got back into my car and used my instinct to guide me back across Bradford to the photography studio, where I arrived 15 minutes before my partner was due to finish his photography course. AMAZING!

Many people would have had negative feelings about the fact that the course was so far away from home. For some couples, it might have been the cause of an argument or even a request that the partner didn't go on the course at all. Remember this story when someone else arranges something unexpected. Instead of fighting it, try to go with the flow and imagine an AMAZING adventure that is great for you.

It is possible to spend so much time trying to control everything in your life that you prevent life from leading you to AMAZING surprises. If you feel your life is mundane, it is probably because you are not allowing things to happen to you. You can rectify this right now by feeling the AMAZING feeling of a bright future. Soon, AMAZING things will start happening to you.

Get into the AMAZING zone and feel AMAZING.

Chapter summary

✁ Add the word AMAZING to your everyday vocabulary.

✁ Write the word AMAZING in your everyday life.

✁ Use the pebbles-in-the-pond technique: imagine the pebbles represent any negatives in your mind, then throw them into the garden pond and let them dissolve.

✁ Feel optimistic about things working out AMAZINGLY well.

✁ Say 'AMAZING. It's AMAZING. It's working out AMAZINGLY well. It has worked out AMAZINGLY well.'

✁ Use the stepping-stone technique: imagine your life is a series of stepping stones that are the solid ground of the past behind you and the future ahead.

✁ Speak positively to yourself.

✁ The sooner you start focusing on the life you want, the sooner you will be living that life.

✁ Use the AMAZING day technique: SMILE as you fall asleep at bedtime and imagine each day is AMAZING.

✁ You might be very good in some areas of your life but not in others. Cutting the negative and getting into the AMAZING zone will help you to change this.

✂ Let life be an AMAZING adventure.

✂ Take a snapshot in your mind of AMAZING moments happening in your life.

✂ Bank good experiences into your AMAZING zone.

✂ Don't buy into negative dramas. Instead, say 'Cut the crap and feel AMAZING.'

STEP 1. Rise above the drama.

STEP 2. Presume it will work out AMAZINGLY well.

STEP 3. Say 'AMAZING'.

*Your SMILE is the most AMAZING tool
you have to improve your life.
It is free and you carry it with you wherever you go.
Raise the corners of your mouth into a
SMILE and feel even more AMAZING.*

CHAPTER 2

SMILE

Many years ago, I was reading a book on how to meditate. As you can imagine, it is difficult to meditate whilst reading a book! I thought there must be an easier way to do it. So I put the book down, closed my eyes and asked myself what would be the easiest, best, most powerful, most AMAZING meditation technique. And then, in a light-bulb moment, I got the answer: just SMILE.

To strengthen the AMAZING zone, I teach clients my SMILE technique. When you SMILE your brain produces a chemical – called dopamine – that lifts your spirits to create positive, happy feelings.

You can SMILE at any time and in any place. Just relax and raise the corners of your mouth into a SMILE. As soon as you do this, you will start to feel happy feelings, your body will become physically more relaxed and you will feel better emotionally too.

I have used this technique with many of my clients to dissolve depression or negative feelings. It is difficult to feel down when you are smiling, especially when your brain is telling you that you feel good. When you SMILE you will notice that your mind becomes solution-focused, so you can work out the best way to approach everyday problems, which in turn will help you to create a great future.

There are two ways I teach this:

1. SMILE technique

Simply SMILE doing everyday things such as brushing your teeth, working, doing the housework, tidying up, reading a book, walking around the supermarket, driving the car or studying. Allow yourself to think things through while you are smiling. You will notice you feel more positive.

2. SMILE meditation

Close your eyes when you are relaxed in a suitable place, such as in bed, on the sofa, sitting on a train or in a plane. SMILE and allow the positive feelings to wash over you. While you are smiling, think about your life and about something you want to achieve. You will automatically feel that it is achievable. Let any frustrated or negative feelings pass. Everything will seem better when you are smiling. You will feel things soften and they won't seem so bad. Not only will it make you feel better at the time, it will also build a bank of positive feelings to help you create a more positive future.

I suggest that you test the SMILE technique for yourself. Try thinking of a problem without smiling and then SMILE and think of the same problem. As soon as you SMILE, you will feel solution-focused and much more positive about the situation. For example:

Without a SMILE someone may feel: worried and stressed about money.

With a SMILE they will feel: my finances are manageable and I will find a way to get through this.

By doing the SMILE technique you will find it easier to create AMAZING feelings. You will also realize that you don't have to take life so seriously. The more you SMILE, the happier and healthier you will feel.

Maybe a lack of smiling is partly why there are so many people turning to anti-depressants – because they are not producing enough 'happy chemicals'. Think of your daily SMILE as your natural anti-depressant.

Depression and stress are learned in childhood when children are put under too much pressure to perform in a certain way – 'Sit here. Do this. Be quiet.' From an early age, people are going against their instincts and against what feels natural and right for them. Young children naturally SMILE, but once they go to school they sit at desks with serious faces, and I believe this is when depression begins to form, as it goes against their natural state of being. Rules and regulations are necessary for discipline and structure, but children need to express themselves through the activities that resonate with them as individuals.

I had the opportunity to visit Nigeria in 2004. During my time there, I did some art therapy with children at an orphanage. The children lived in a small, cramped house, slept on the floor at night, and didn't eat every day as there wasn't always food. Their ages ranged from 3 to 18. From an outsider's perspective, they had very little, if anything, to be happy about. But they had the most incredibly positive spirits and a joy that sang from their hearts in a way I have never seen in children in the UK.

At first I couldn't put my finger on what was creating the happiness in the children in the orphanage. Then I realized that it was their sense of freedom. They were creative with the art, which they enjoyed enormously. Later during the same trip, I went into a British International School with the same art materials. This time, the children were more reserved, waiting for approval and instructions about what to do with the art materials. Pegged to a piece of string was a row of paintings of ladybirds, all of which were identical – even the spots were in the same places.

The children at the International School looked a bit depressed in comparison to the children at the orphanage. And I realized that the education system was crushing the joy out of them. Standardizing their artwork reduced it to nothing more than a manufactured line of pointless paintings. Expressing ourselves is a natural process, which we need to do to be happy. As Western children grow up, their lives become less expressive and more controlled. By the time they reach adulthood, the cracks have begun to show and, for some people, accumulated lack of freedom and too much conforming will eventually lead to a midlife crisis.

Learn to feel the AMAZING SMILEY feelings that will enable you to move on to better things and enjoy what you are doing. It will help you to make good choices to improve your life.

By beginning to SMILE more in your everyday life and by using the SMILE meditation as an exercise to create positive feelings, you can start to rekindle the flames of the joyful feelings that may have been extinguished in your early childhood. The SMILE exercise is good for everyone and can help people release depressed and anxious feelings. Start by smiling little and often until you get used to smiling regularly again.

Remember, you can't change the people around you, but by changing the way you feel, people will respond to you differently. When you are happier, you will radiate a more positive energy, which other people will pick up on. Some people won't want to be in your positive space, but it will appeal to others. Your new positivity may not suit all your friends, so allow your relationships to evolve naturally as people come in and out of your life.

Even for people who say, 'I SMILE a lot already,' using the SMILE more will create even better things.

Be nice to other people, but don't get caught up in their dramas or negativity. Realize that they are in a negative place and perhaps suggest some of the techniques for them to try or that they read this book. But remember, not everyone is ready for change, so don't be a rescuer. Other people's negativity will prevent you from feeling the

AMAZING feelings. So teach people to take responsibility for themselves.

Although you can't run and hide from all the negative things going on in the world, you *can* see negativity for what it is, step back from it and not allow it to get into your body. There is always a positive that can come out of something. So presume AMAZING things will happen as a result – you don't need to know what, when or how.

Remember that there is always going to be someone worse off than you are. Instead of dwelling on that fact, do your bit to make a positive difference to the world. A kind gesture can go a long way in the day of a real person. Talking to an elderly person can make them less lonely. Putting money in a charity box will make a difference to someone somewhere. Noticing something good about your wife or husband and mentioning it to them will make your relationship happier.

SMILE and spend a few minutes every day laughing at life, loving where you are and accepting it. Once you can see the funny side, you will already have begun to change your life for the better. You can carry a SMILE wherever you go.

Laugh at life and feel AMAZING.

Chapter summary

✂ Strengthen the AMAZING zone with a SMILE.

✂ Do something every week that really makes you SMILE.

✂ Be kind to yourself and other people.

✂ Let your uniqueness shine.

STEP 1. Raise the corners of your mouth into a SMILE.

STEP 2. SMILE as you do everyday tasks.

STEP 3. Think things through with a SMILE.

Every challenge has already been overcome by someone somewhere. You can do it too.

CHAPTER 3

CUT THE CRAP AND LET GO OF WORRIES

Let go of the negative and make way for the positive

To be able to create positive, happy feelings you have to let go of negative feelings. We all worry about something, get stressed or have negative thoughts at some point. One of the first things I teach clients is to take control of their spiralling negative thoughts, which cause anxiety and stress and which occupy time that could be used positively. As what we 'think' is who we are or who we become, it is really important that you use positive words when you are thinking. The sooner you improve the way you think, the sooner you will change your life positively.

If you have a dispute with a neighbour and, instead of dwelling on the stress or feeling trapped because you think there is nothing you can do, you focus on it working out well, it is more likely to be sorted out. Being positive will give you the energy to get advice and gather together all the information that will make a difference. Rather than feeling tired, drained and helpless, let the situation empower you so that AMAZING solutions can be found.

You may have experienced challenging times that you feel you can't easily move on from. With some information and understanding about how the events occurred, it will be easier to put them behind you. Or you may have negative thoughts simply because you are dealing with difficult everyday problems. Depression and down feelings are partly the result of dwelling on the past or feeling trapped in life, allowing the mind to rethink events over and over again. They also occur when your subconscious mind, your conscious mind and your reality do not match.

- 'If only that had happened or this hadn't happened.'

- 'Life was so much better back then.'

- 'I should be doing better than I am doing. I was expecting to be Y and I have only achieved X.'

Some of these beliefs will have been drilled into you by society, parents, schooling, films and, basically, just life around you. Anti-depressants will mask your negative feelings, but they won't change your beliefs. Changing your life little by little will get you out of a negative rut. Even if you are taking anti-depressants, you can still change your life and then work with your doctor later to come off them, if that's appropriate. This technique helps prevent people from slipping into hopeless feelings.

Climbing-out-of-a-hole technique

To help release the feeling of being stuck in life or having low or depressed feelings, you can visualize yourself climbing out of a dark hole into the light. See it as a cartoon computer game, as if you are reaching the next level of lightness. Keep climbing into the light until you feel you are surrounded by light in your mind.

This visualization will help you to look for the way through whatever you are facing right now. By imagining yourself making progress, you will program your mind to believe that there is a way out of the situation you are in. This will help you to find solutions. You can do this exercise at any time in any place.

Photo album technique

Imagine your past is like a photo album. Don't look at the individual pictures, just see a collection of photos in your mind. Now imagine archiving the images into folders. Imagine the past events being filed away into a place that feels fine. Imagine the images moving into the relevant folders. It may feel right to let some of the photos and folders dissolve and disappear. Again, don't look at the pictures. Just trust that they are going into the correct places. See the images in your mind sorting themselves out. As you do this exercise, let go of the past knowing that everything is in place for you to move your life forwards positively. Visualize a blank new photo album that you can fill with images of all your future adventures. Repeat the exercise at any time when you feel yourself dwelling on the past.

I had a client who couldn't come to terms with her children leaving home. She had too many happy memories of being a full-time mum. By doing this exercise, she felt that she had filed the photos of the past away and freed her mind so that she could plan her future and move on to the next exciting chapter of her life.

Getting back to being whole and complete

For argument's sake, let's imagine you were whole and complete when you were born into the world. Imagine yourself at birth being like a complete circle. Then life began to chip away at you – teachers, tests, exams, parents, siblings, expectations and disappointments – until eventually you weren't a perfect circle any more, and you weren't your true self any more either. You were a lesser version of you, and the circle had begun to look a bit distorted and misshapen.

Every time you had to sit in a classroom learning information that didn't really make sense to you or that appeared to have no relevance to your life, every time you were misunderstood or felt awkward and self-conscious, the circle got a little bit more bent out of shape. Eventually, you began to negatively self-talk.

- 'I am stupid.'

- 'What's wrong with me?'

You may have worried about specific things, played up or been rude, or you may have had low self-esteem, because your instinct was saying one thing while life and the people around you were saying something else. Then the inner battle with yourself began and every bad feeling masked the true, happy you. You stopped using your instinct, which was prompting you to do the right things. Instead, you followed half-hearted feelings or opted for safe options. Perhaps other people persuaded you against making the right decisions at times. Sometimes you were able to follow your instinct, but at other times you questioned your decisions and learned to go against what felt right for you. And you learned to feel bad about what you were doing.

The good news is that you can change all this. It was your thinking that bent the circle, and it is your thinking that can make it circular again. It is time to get back to your true self and take back control of your mind. Remember that other people who bully, argue, annoy, self-doubt, are rude or jealous behave that way because they have experienced the same inner turmoil. Observe negative people and understand that they have their own problems or issues to deal with, which make them the way they are.

- STOP taking things personally: other people are in a troubled place too.

- STOP letting other people put you down and START believing in yourself more.

- Everyone is doing the best they can with the knowledge and personality they have. It may not be great, but it is the best they can do.

- Be around people who are right for you.

- Many of your personal characteristics and parts of your life are great, but an improved version of you would be AMAZING.

- Remember the good things you were taught at school, such as discipline, being focused and being able to follow a routine. Keep the good things and change the things you don't like.

Worries or fears may arise from time to time. Sometimes we have to work them out. At other times, worrying is unnecessary and doesn't help at all.

Whenever you have a negative thought, you could do the following techniques to prevent your feelings spiralling out of control. If we hold on to a thought and turn it over and over in our mind, it will become like tangled washing in a washing machine. Try to stop the bad thoughts as soon as they arise.

- Accept that bad thoughts are there, deal with them and let them pass.

The thoughts in your head may be: 'I feel rubbish. I hate myself. Life is unfair.'

The answer in your head could be: 'Great. AMAZING. That's fine. But now I choose to let those thoughts pass by like clouds in the sky.'

I teach these exercises to all my clients to help them control their feelings. Try using them regularly whenever you find yourself worrying, feeling nervous, anxious, hyperactive, stressed or being negative.

Clouds-in-the-sky technique
To release negative thoughts or worry, use the fingers of your right hand to rub, tap or press the knuckles of your

left hand to reassure yourself that everything will be fine. You can do this subtly in front of other people – if you clasp your hands, no one will notice you rubbing, tapping or pressing your knuckles. Say to yourself, 'Let it go. Let it pass.' Imagine the bad feeling passing by. Thoughts are fluid, moving objects that will pass like clouds drift across the sky if you allow them to do so. Repeat the exercise until the bad feelings pass and repeat it regularly throughout the day to ward off anxious or worried feelings.

Red triangle technique

Visualize a red triangle in your mind. Put the negative thoughts, fears, bad feelings, uncomfortable emotions, paranoid thoughts, bad habits and stress into the triangle. Then imagine the triangle shrinking until it is as small as a speck of dust. Then imagine blowing the speck of dust away. As the triangle disappears, you will create space for AMAZING solutions to reveal themselves to you during the coming days and weeks. You can say to yourself, 'I am safe. It's going to be fine.' Repeat this exercise as often as you want. Presume that, from today, good things will come and people will have good things to say about you.

• LIBERATE yourself by letting go of past grudges, worries and anxieties using the above techniques. Most things are not important.

Anxiety is fear of the future: 'What if something bad happens?'

I teach clients, 'What if something AMAZING happens? What if it turns out to be the best thing?'

The next time you worry about the future, joke to yourself, 'What if it is the most AMAZING thing?' and SMILE.

If something doesn't happen, assume that something better will happen instead.

If something goes wrong, embrace it, love it like a favourite pet: feel good about it and it will turn into something better.

If you are worried about someone else, assume that things will work out AMAZINGLY well for them.

Always feel the feeling of things having worked out AMAZINGLY well. This will enable you to bypass any negative worries or concerns, which in turn will keep you feeling better within yourself. Anxiety results from allowing the negative thoughts to spiral. So rein them in and try to feel positive feelings.

Another technique is to imagine celebrating as if future events have already gone AMAZINGLY well.

A client of mine was worrying herself into a state of frenzy about her daughter going away on a school trip on a coach. I got her to visualize her daughter stepping off the bus after the trip, safe, smiling and having had a nice time. It made the mother feel instantly in control and relaxed about her child. Using this 'after the event' visualization technique also made a massive difference to her life in general.

Another client was worried that his house would flood during a period of extremely heavy rain. I used the techniques in this book with him to release his anxieties and told him to imagine that it had all worked out AMAZINGLY well. He imagined the floods had gone and his house had remained dry the whole time. When he came back a few weeks later, he said that his house was one of very few properties in the village that had not been flooded and he told me, 'It is AMAZING!'

When it comes to local and world news, imagine all the issues in the world sorting out AMAZINGLY well. Throughout history, people all over the world have overcome all sorts of problems. I watch the news to know what is going on, but I don't allow myself to get caught up in the negative drama.

Whatever the results of an election or referendum, I presume that it will all work out in the end. Perhaps the events will lead eventually to better outcomes, maybe five or 10 years down the line. Whatever is happening in the news learn to manage your mind and your feelings. Remember, the news doesn't include all the good things that are happening around the world. So don't focus on the things that don't work. Instead, think about all the people who are working hard to make a real difference to other people's lives on a daily basis.

Feel good about things and imagine positive outcomes. Use the SMILE technique to help you feel good feelings. Speak a positive language in your head and run a positive film of events in your mind.

If someone is going on a plane journey, imagine they have arrived at their destination safe and well, or have returned home safely after their holiday, and that they are back at home telling you about their AMAZING trip. Imagine them in bed, safe and sound.

If you are applying for a job, imagine you are already working in that job. If you don't get that job, do the same with the next one you apply for. Feel the feeling of doing the journey to and from that place of work. Eventually, with this positive attitude, you will get an AMAZING job.

If you worry about your children, feel the feeling of them being grown-up and happy in their lives, doing AMAZING jobs, having AMAZING relationships and living in AMAZING homes.

If you worry about socialising or meeting people, imagine the event has gone AMAZINGLY well, feel the feeling of returning home with a smile on your face as you are pleased with the way the meeting has gone. Speak reassuring words to yourself: 'I am fine. This is fine. I am pleasant company to be with and people like me.'

If you worry about paying your bills or about being in debt, feel the feeling of having extra money every month and AMAZING savings in the bank.

If you worry about your investments, feel the feeling of making good investment decisions and of everything working out AMAZINGLY well.

If you worry about health issues, imagine them working out AMAZINGLY well so that you and your loved ones are fit and healthy. When things do go well, remember to snapshot them in your mind to build your AMAZING zone bank.

It is sometimes hard for people to visualize a positive future. The following exercise will help.

Wiggly string technique

Visualize the future as being like a wiggly string leading you on an AMAZING treasure hunt through your life. Imagine the string going in different directions: it wiggles to the left and to the right, down and up, and it leads you to the things you need to find. Let your life be an adventure. This exercise will help you to flow and be flexible in your attitudes to life. Trust that AMAZING things can happen. When you believe there is going to be a way forward, you will find it.

When you are worried about the future or dragged down by the past, you don't feel free and comfortable in the present. Being in the present time requires you to see the past as the strong foundation on which you have built the person you are and the future as the adventure that lies ahead of you. Say to yourself, 'Life is an AMAZING adventure.'

You can come to terms with really terrible times if you focus more on the good feelings and less on the bad. You have already started the process of change by reading this chapter. The techniques will allow your mind to let go of the past and create positive new thinking.

You can't always change a situation quickly. Change may take some time. So keep making good choices and decisions and feel AMAZING about it eventually working out AMAZINGLY well.

See past events as stepping stones in your mind, part of the journey and foundation of your strength. We develop our characteristics from our life experiences. Without the bad things, we wouldn't be able to appreciate the good. Embrace your past as part of the good in your life today.

There is always a positive that can come from a negative experience, even if it is only that you can help one other person as a result of your knowledge. I believe that has got to be a good thing.

Cut the negative from your life and feel AMAZING.

Chapter summary

✂ It is not what is happening but how you respond to it that is important.

✂ Use the climbing-out-of-a-hole technique: visualize yourself climbing into the light.

✂ Use the photo album technique: imagine the past stored in photo albums.

✂ You can't change the past, but you can change the way you feel about the past.

✂ Soften your reaction to the past and to the future by SMILING and accepting.

✂ Use the clouds-in-the-sky technique: let worries pass like clouds moving across the sky and rub, press or tap your knuckles to reassure yourself.

✂ Cut the worries from your life and feel AMAZING.

✂ Imagine it is a year from now and you have had an AMAZING year.

✂ Use the red triangle technique: visualize a red triangle, put your worries into it and then shrink it down.

✂ Use the wiggly string technique: imagine the future as being like a wiggly string leading you on an AMAZING adventure.

STEP 1. Identify the negative.

STEP 2. Consciously let the negative go.

STEP 3. Say, 'What if it is AMAZING?'

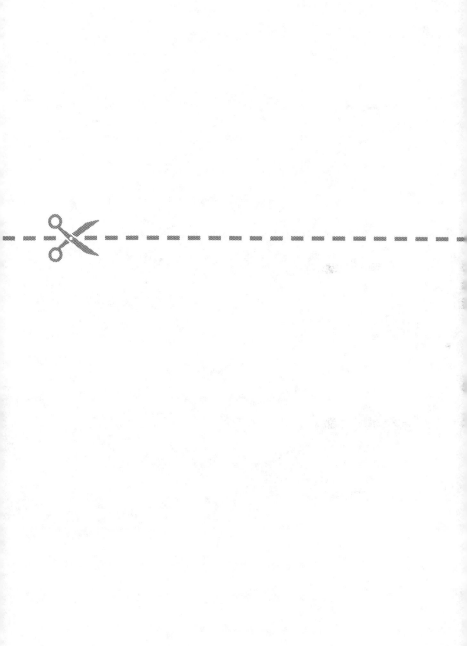

*By making good choices and decisions,
you can create an AMAZING life.
What are you waiting for?*

CHAPTER 4

CHOICES AND DECISIONS

If you analyse your life, you will realize that it is just a series of choices and decisions, large and small. Those choices and decisions are the building blocks with which you create the person you are and the life you are living. By understanding this, you can begin to make better choices and decisions on a daily basis to improve your life. As a child, you weren't in control of choices and decisions, but as an adult you are. Making good small choices will lead you to bigger positive outcomes.

If you feel trapped because you think you are too far off the path of the life you want to live, realize that it is only a state of mind making you feel this way. Right here, right now, you can begin to change your life by making better decisions. When you do, you will be able to see how all your past choices and decisions led you to where you are now.

- **Regularly making small better choices and decisions will get you back on course for an AMAZING life.**

Don't leap out of the life you are in and run away from it. Instead, start to make different choices that will improve your day, your week, your relationships and eventually your whole life. As you gradually make the changes, you will begin to see improvements. Some things will turn out fine, others may never do so. But always make decisions when you are in a good place within yourself, otherwise you may run from one bad situation to another that is different but equally as bad.

If you don't enjoy your job, drive to work by a different route or get there early and go for a coffee before you start your day. Or avoid the rush hour after work by going for a swim while the traffic dies down – you may get home a bit later, but at least you will be relaxed. There is no rule that says you have to drive home when everyone else does. You do it simply because that's what most other people do.

Instead of feeling frustrated by your commute, SMILE and make positive statements such as, 'I have an AMAZING journey. I have an AMAZING lifestyle.' Your mind will listen to the words you speak and you will then make the changes necessary to create an AMAZING lifestyle. But if you moan in your head, repeating angry or frustrated comments, you will drag yourself down and your mind will give you more negative things to moan about. A few tweaks to your daily routine will enhance your week:

- A positive state of mind will help you make better choices and decisions.

- Choosing to do things differently in your day will make you feel better about what you are doing and your day will go better.

Choose not to react to bad news. Instead, remember all the good, kind things that are happening in the world.

A good example of this is when the British TV personality Jade Goody sadly passed away from cervical cancer in March 2009 at the young age of 27. Jade had won the hearts of the nation when she took part in the Channel 4 TV reality show, Big Brother, in 2002, after which she went on to star in several television programmes of her own.

In 2007, she returned to the celebrity version of Big Brother, during which her celebrity turned to notoriety when she became involved in a racial bullying incident with the Indian actress Shilpa Shetty. Afterwards Jade apologized and in August 2008 she appeared on the Indian version of Big Brother called Big Boss. It was during the live programme that Jade was told she had cervical cancer and when she subsequently returned to the UK, she discovered that the cancer was terminal. After her diagnosis, Jade continued to live a very public life, even allowing a film crew to follow her cancer journey for the documentary *Jade's Cancer Battle*.

Many people had followed Jade's story on the television and watched her undergo hospital treatment, and many felt they knew her. After she died, I had an influx of clients who were traumatized by her death and I told them, 'Something good always comes from everything. Yes, it is tragic for Jade and her family. But the people who loved her should be very proud of her because she was brave enough to share her story and will save many other lives. In fact, hundreds of women who had never bothered to have cervical screening tests came forwards after Jade's death to be screened. In the long term, Jade will continue to help other women who will now live to see their children grow up. If you look at the bigger picture, you will see that, even when we can't control things, there is always a positive in everything.

Try to be an optimist so that you make better choices and decisions about how you react to the events that occur around you. For example, if someone loses their job, try to find the positive and presume they will find a better one. If you have a rotten weekend, maybe because you have a hangover or are tired from a late night drinking, you could plan an alcohol-free weekend when you could go to a spa, go sailing or go-karting or even hire a Porsche and go for a drive. It doesn't matter what you do. How you spend your time is your choice. But don't repeat old behaviour and do the thing that drags you down. It sounds obvious, but it often isn't to people who are caught up in the routine of their lives.

- Don't do the same thing and expect a different result.

- Instead, do different things and get different results.

- Even better, do AMAZING things and get AMAZING results.

If the children are tiring you out, plan downtime activities such as a home cinema, curtains closed, with a bucket of popcorn that, ideally, they have made with you. Or get them to help you make and pack up a picnic, then go to the park and let them run around and entertain themselves while you relax.

If you are tired or stressed, choose to have a relaxing weekend. Plan ahead and make conscious choices and decisions that will improve your weekend. Start to take control of all your choices and decisions. Ask yourself what you could do differently.

- You don't need to be a slave to your children.

- You don't need to be a slave to your day.

- You don't need to be a slave to your work.

- You don't need to be a slave to your partner, family or friends.

A client of mine was living away from home during the week in a cheap hotel that wasn't very nice. He was a bit depressed, so he was drinking alcohol every night to drown his sorrows. I asked him, 'Why do you battle through the traffic to get back to an empty hotel room? Why don't you go out somewhere after work and have a coffee while you read the newspaper, or even for an inexpensive dinner? While everyone else is fighting their way through the traffic, you could be relaxing and enjoying your evenings. Then, by the time you get back to the hotel, you won't feel the need to have a drink. You could have a bath or shower and then watch something interesting on the TV.' He came back a few weeks later having made the changes and told me that his life was very different and he was feeling much better. So small changes really can make a massive difference to the enjoyment of your week.

Use your instinct to make good choices and decisions and be creative. Sometimes, fear gets in the way. So identify whether it is the fear of being taken out of your comfort zone that is stopping you doing something, or whether there is a genuine risk that you need to avoid. If you can't make a decision about something, it might not be the right day to decide. And that's okay – just put the issue on a shelf in your mind and go back to it another day. By the time you return to it, you may have more information that will enable you to make the right choice.

Sometimes, people want to leave a job and do something else, but what they may do is simply create the same problems all over again. Identify why you want to change things and what you could do better. Before you change your job, ask yourself the following questions, which will help you to make the right choices.

- What skills do I have?

- How much time have I invested in learning what I know?

- How can I apply these skills somewhere else?

- What are the benefits for me continuing to do what I do now?

- What have I achieved so far?

- If I don't change my job, how could I enjoy my day better or feel better about myself?

Taking care of yourself in your home life will help you to be less tired at work and to enjoy your job more. You will feel less tired if you enjoy your journey to and from work, take a lunch break, eat nutritious meals and drink sips of water throughout the day.

There are all sorts of things you can do to improve your

job and the way you feel about work. You may even start to look for a promotion or another position within the company where you are already working. Or you may feel that it is time for a career change, which you can begin to plan and prepare for calmly.

Many of my clients have gone on to love jobs they previously hated, because it wasn't the job that needed changing but their attitude and lifestyle. Some of them changed their jobs later, but the transition was more positive and smoother than it might otherwise have been, because they felt better about themselves.

Feel AMAZING as you enjoy each part of each day more and more, knowing that if change is the answer, you will move smoothly in the right direction. Your biggest asset is yourself, who you are and the skills you have. So don't throw it all into the bin and have to start again unnecessarily. Build upon what you have already achieved. By making better choices and decisions, you will guide your life in the right direction. Every time there is a brick wall in front of you, remember to make new choices and decisions so that you can navigate your way around it.

If you have problems at home, start to work out what those problems are so that you can manage them. If you are arguing with your partner or your kids, or if you don't have a partner, or you have lost a partner, start to think about what you could do differently.

Do as much as you can to change the way you feel about where you are rather than running away from your life. Change your interaction with yourself and with other people by being more positive. As you feel better and more relaxed, you will become better company to be with and you will be able to bring the good out of others, too. You may feel that other people won't change, but if you SMILE and imagine things have already gone AMAZINGLY well, you may be surprised by what happens.

For example, I had a client who visited an old family friend who was normally very negative. My client saw her out of duty rather than enjoyment. She usually dreaded going to visit her. But then, one day, she made the choice of imagining herself coming out of her friend's house after lunch having had an AMAZING time. And that's exactly what happened. Her friend only spoke of positive things and they had a lovely lunch together with lots of laughter, which my client had never experienced with her friend before.

- **AMAZING choices and decisions will help you feel more in control of your life.**

It is all about making small changes in your day. If you are at your desk and you are bored or stressed or have too much to get done, think, 'How could I tackle this differently?' Make different choices and decisions and most of the problems in your life will start to dissolve, simply because you feel different as a result of making different choices.

If it is all kicking off at work or at home, just say, 'AMAZING. AMAZING. Fantastic. This is AMAZING.' Feel the feeling of making the right choices and decisions to get you out of the situation. You may feel frustrated, but let it pass. By getting into the habit of rising above issues, you will deal with things better. For example, if you have a difficult neighbour or boss to deal with, just say: 'AMAZING. I will find solutions to dealing with this situation.' Feel good about the situation resolving.

One of the reasons it is AMAZING is because you are identifying the problem so that you can resolve it. Use the SMILE technique so that you can laugh at the situation. By feeling AMAZING or fantastic, you are already feeling better.

Once you feel better, you will turn it into a better situation. SMILE and imagine things have resolved AMAZINGLY well. Feel the good celebration feeling inside you as if it has all worked out well.

Your life may be so busy that you haven't had the brain space to work things out. Or you may have been programming yourself with the same limiting thoughts that have stopped you being able to see things differently. When people go on holiday, they are able to see their lives with fresh eyes. Usually, that makes them feel a bit better about things because they can see where to make adjustments on their return home. This is because they have more brain space while they are away.

I teach clients an exercise to help massage out those stuck, rigid choices and decisions. It's really like a massage in your mind. The exercise is incredibly powerful, easy to do at any time and makes a massive difference by enabling you to let go of trapped, stuck and overloaded feelings. This technique will help you to make constant adjustments to keep your life flowing.

Music control-settings technique

Imagine your mind and your life being like a music technician's control panel in a recording studio, with lots of sliding buttons and switches that flick on and off. Imagine all those different control settings now, as you think about the area of your life you want to work on. Go to this part of the control panel and slide the settings up and down as you imagine this area of your life adjusting positively. Move the sliders as you feel good about positive changes happening. Adjust the settings as you feel good about your life becoming harmonious. As the settings adjust, glide the slider buttons in different ways. Switch some of them off if you like. Just do what feels right in your own creative way. By tweaking the settings slightly here and there, the small adjustments will help you to create new choices and decisions. Close your eyes if you want to. It's like having a massage in your mind and a massage in your life, making you feel better.

Imagine each area of your life is represented by a certain area of the control panel. Visualize as best you can doing some work in a particular area by moving the controls, adjusting and resetting them until you feel relaxed. You will find that if you do this exercise regularly, your mind will start to change, allowing you to come up with more solutions for yourself. You will feel differently about things that previously caused tension and stress. Things that used to seem impossible will resolve.

You can use the technique at any time. When you wake up in the morning, imagine the settings adjusting your day so that it works out well. Do the exercise on the way to work, in a traffic jam, waiting for a bus, when you go to the toilet or during any spare moment you have. After a while, it will become second nature to you, as your mind processes everything smoothly. Used regularly, it will help unlock your mind from the old, bad habits by tweak, tweak, tweaking the settings of your emotions, stresses, work, confidence issues, worries, money and relationships.

Be creative in your day. Be creative in your week. Be creative in your weekend. Don't just do what you did yesterday, last week, last weekend, or what you think you should be doing because of your age group or your circumstances. At school you had to fit the mould of what was expected of you and generally do what everyone else was doing. But you are not at school now. So be very creative with your time. Be individual.

Often clients ask me, 'How can I fill my weekend with

positive things? What is there to do? There is nothing to do.' And I tell them, 'If you look around where you are right now, there are so many things to do. There are people out there doing all sorts of activities, gardening, walking a dog (borrow a dog if you need to), going to local cafés, joining clubs, reading, researching topics of interest, going to galleries and museums, starting courses online or at colleges.'

If you have children, do things with them that are relevant to their age group so that you can enjoy your time as a family at each stage of their lives. Get to know what's available in your local area. We live in a country that has so many opportunities and so many activities that are free that you will be able to find something to do, whatever your budget.

Start your Monday morning by saying, 'Wow, I had an AMAZING weekend. It was fantastic. I went on a course and met some AMAZING people.' Listen to what you think, feel and say about your weekend.

Already your life has begun to change. When you start to make better choices and decisions, your world will open up and great things will happen. You can strengthen your choices and decisions by combining them with AMAZING phrases such as, 'I am making AMAZING choices and decisions,' and 'I make AMAZING things happen.' To begin with, it may feel as though you are just playing a game, but you will soon see positive results.

Your progress in life is not something that is happening outside of yourself. It is happening inside you. Your words and actions command the direction you are going in every moment of every day as your subconscious mind absorbs the information you program into it. It all begins with you. You are in control. The more you use these techniques, the faster you will see change in your life.

I tell all my clients that change is the most important

thing: CHANGE, CHANGE, CHANGE, CHANGE, CHANGE. So start changing how you see things, and remember that all things are possible.

Every time you write a negative review, you are sending out a negative message about who you are. Instead, write constructive suggestions to a company that's got something wrong and give them the chance to improve before posting a public complaint. Most businesses work hard to provide good products and services for their clients. If they don't always get things right, it's worth remembering that their staff are only human and they might simply have made a mistake. Even better, rather than focusing on saying negative things about your experiences, choose to write positive reviews about companies who get things right. Send a thank-you card to a business that is doing something well and thank local businesses for the services they provide to the people living in your area. Your attitude is creating your experience. If you home in on the bad, you will get more of it. It's a bit like Karma – what you give out comes back.

Use your instinct about what feels right rather than being influenced by a negative person's point of view on a review. More 'negative' types of people write reviews than positive people. The positive people are too busy getting on with living a great life. Let your instinct lead you to a great place to eat as you make life an adventure through good choices and decisions. When you make happy choices and decisions, you will find yourself in the right place at the right time.

Cut the boring routine from your life and feel AMAZING.

Chapter summary

✂ Regular small changes will help you make bigger changes.

✂ Be creative about how you live your life.

✂ Make choices and decisions when you feel balanced and in a good frame of mind.

✂ AMAZING choices and decisions will create AMAZING outcomes.

✂ Make your life interesting and varied.

✂ Every choice and decision made by you or by other people has got you to where you are. You can now take control by making better choices and decisions that will get you to where you want to go.

✂ Use the music control-settings technique: visualize the settings of a control panel and adjust them to improve each area of your life.

✂ Write a list of pros and cons to help you make decisions.

✂ Use your instinct to make choices and decisions combined with your business head.

STEP 1. Identify what you would like to improve.

STEP 2. Think of ways to improve it.

STEP 3. Remember to make AMAZING choices and decisions from now onwards.

If everyone did what was right for them,
people would be more accomplished.
Anyone can achieve something they believe in.

CHAPTER 5

I CAN DO IT

I can do it. I am doing it. It is done.

Everyone has felt stuck or unmotivated about something at some point. You may have things you need to do right now or goals you want to achieve, but you may not be able to get started or see a way of achieving the bigger goals.

Black/white/grey thinking

People tend to see things as either black or white and fail to realize that there is a whole grey area in between the two, which is where all the solutions are.

An example of black-and-white thinking is:

- black = someone wants to change their job but they can't see how to do it so they automatically think…

- white = 'I have to stay here' or 'It is too difficult to get a new job'…

- whereas the answers lie within the grey area, where the solutions are…

- grey = they could start looking for other job options, or investigate new training, or apply for some jobs.

It's a good idea to look for one thing in the grey area that will help you to achieve whatever it is you are trying to do. Seeing everything as either black or white can make you feel stuck, and when you feel stuck you may procrastinate and end up doing nothing at all. Often, thinking about doing something is more taxing than actually doing it, particularly when 'doing it' simply involves picking up the phone and getting it sorted out. Look for all the available options. Be creative when looking for answers. And, from now on, remember the grey area.

You can use the information in this chapter on a daily basis, as well as to improve a particular area of your life. Keep your life moving in the direction you want it to go and don't be put off by small limiting thoughts.

For instance, instead of thinking, 'I can't afford the house I want so I am stuck here forever,' you could expand your property search to include some of the many other, equally good, streets that you could afford to live in. Or you could find a way to save more money so that you can buy the house you want. Or buy it with a friend. Or get a better-paid job to improve your financial situation. Once you start looking for solutions in the grey area and taking action, you will start making progress and, before you know it, you will be moving to your new home.

You don't need to be able to see around the next corner from where you stand now. You just need to get to the corner. When you do, seeing around it and knowing what your next step needs to be will be easy. Imagine the AMAZING feeling of standing in your new home, holding the new keys in your hand. You don't need to know which home it is, just that it's one you love and that it's AMAZING.

Another example of a limiting thought is, 'I don't know everything that I am supposed to be revising. I am completely useless.' Remember that no one knows everything. Everyone has their own strengths and weaknesses and by doing your best, you will probably do well enough. Even if you don't pass, you could retake the exam, or find a better path for yourself. Being aware that the grey area exists will help you put things in perspective and make you more likely to look for solutions and to do whatever needs to be done to help yourself.

I have helped lots of students to adopt an 'I can do it' attitude. By saying to yourself, 'I can do it. I am doing it. It is done,' and feeling the AMAZING feeling of holding your result paper and being happy with it, you will achieve your goals.

It is helpful when having conversations with other people to notice when they are being black and white in their thinking and not seeing the grey area between the two. Looking for solutions to their problems will help you to be creative in finding solutions for yourself.

When people live in a black-and-white world without the grey, it makes them frustrated and causes them a lot of stress, which can be avoided simply by seeing the grey solutions. When you are speaking to yourself, be aware that there are always solutions to every problem: you just need to look for them in the grey middle ground.

Black = 'The election or referendum has turned out this way so I feel worried, stressed and upset.'

White = 'This is a disaster.'

Grey = 'I could change my conversation with myself. There has to be a positive way through this. I will find what works for me. Perhaps the divided feelings of people will unite everyone in a positive way in the long run. Perhaps there will be good changes as a result of this election or referendum. I can find the AMAZING way through this for myself and my family. It is up to the people of this country to be positive and make sure that this situation works out well.'

Parents often make black-and-white mistakes. For example, when a child says, 'I am going to the party on Saturday,' the parent may respond by saying, 'No, you are not.' What the parent could do instead is remember the grey negotiation area and say, 'Okay, we'll see how your studies go this week,' which diffuses any argument and focuses the child on working hard during the week to earn the right to go out at the weekend.

If you felt trapped as a child in an education system that often put you under pressure, you probably learned that feeling bad about what you are doing is acceptable. When you left school, you did more of what you had learned to do and conformed to things you don't really believe. So when you decide that you want to make something happen, the inner voice of self-doubt may stop you. You need to rise above your past, believe in yourself and say, 'I can do it. I am doing it. It is done.'

There may be an area of your life that you would like to improve. Don't think that you have to be 100% ready to make a change. No one is ever totally sure about something before they start doing it. Striving for perfection can stop you doing anything. So just give new things a go.

Focus on what you want to happen and don't share your ideas with other people, as they may put you off trying. Because we were constantly judged at school, in tests and exams, we are programmed to want the approval of other people. But think outside the box, be yourself and be creative. You are an individual, so trust in yourself and allow your own ideas and personality to help you get on in life. There is not just one way of doing something. Your way will add a sparkle, if you let it. Take control of your mind with an 'I can do it' attitude. Not everything will happen as you expect it to. Some things won't happen at all. But, with a positive, AMAZING attitude, you will be going in the right direction and everything will fall into place along the way.

Thinking differently will get different results

It may be that the change you want to make involves one of the following:

- Get some tasks done at home or at work.

- Get a better job.

- Decorate or tidy your home.

- Move to a better place.

- Study well for an exam.

- Improve a relationship.

- Find a partner.

- Put past events behind you.

- Get your finances sorted out.

- Improve your health.

- Deal with emotional issues.

- Lose weight, stop smoking or reduce the amount of alcohol you drink.

Here are a few pointers to help you get out of the rut:

- Be clear with yourself about what you actually want to achieve.

- Start by doing one thing that will enable you to achieve it.

- Get rid of distractions such as excuses or activities that stop you from achieving your goal: turn off phones, social media, TV and stop listening to other people's problems.

- Use your time wisely.

- Stick to the essentials and don't get sidetracked.

- Remember the determination you had when you were younger and tap into that attitude.

- Wear the sort of clothes that sophisticated, successful people wear so that you feel confident and other people will respect you.

Starting right now, only use positive language about the things you want to change or achieve.

- 'It's all coming together.'

- 'It is working out AMAZINGLY well.'

- 'I am doing it.'

- 'I am AMAZED at how well I have done this.'

- 'It is done.'

Teacher technique

To do this technique, I find that it's a good idea to stand up wherever you are, as you will feel more alert and positive when you are standing rather than slumped in a chair. If you can't stand up, sit as upright as you can on your chair. A positive posture will help you feel more positive in your mind. Raise the corners of your mouth into a gentle SMILE. Imagine the positive 'in-control feeling' of being a positive but firm teacher telling the children what they are going to do. But instead of telling a class of children, you are going to tell yourself what to do.

Think of a goal or something you want to achieve – for example a simple task, a new job, buying a property or passing an exam. Now listen to yourself being the teacher and telling yourself that you are going to do it, that you will do it really well and that you will get it done. Listen to yourself just as you would listen to a teacher. Speak to yourself using your own name, for example, 'Sarah, you will look at some properties. You will look at new areas. You will find a great area to buy in. Sarah, you will register with the estate agents. Sarah, you can get a mortgage. You will look at mortgage options and arrange your mortgage. You will find an AMAZING property and a very good removal company. Sarah, you will find a way to decorate your new home beautifully.' Saying it aloud and listening to yourself will help you to feel that what you are going to do is normal. It will give you confidence and the feeling that everything can be done easily. Don't be shy while practising this at home.

Set yourself time frames, just as you would for lessons, homework, school days and half-terms. Be assertive with yourself. Remember this technique any time you want to get something done and when planning goals. Start by working through each action that needs to be taken to achieve the goal that you have set for yourself. You can use the SMILE technique, as smiling makes you feel more positive, and you can say the word 'AMAZING' while coaching yourself.

Using the word 'perhaps' will also help coax you into doing things. 'Perhaps' takes the pressure off you, because it makes everything sound as though it's optional. 'Perhaps I can do something towards my goal. Perhaps I can do that task. Perhaps I can start and finish this project.'

Feeling satisfied technique

Feel the feeling of accomplishing today's tasks. Feel the satisfied feeling and relief, as if the day has ended well and you have got everything done that you wanted to do. Visualize yourself with the end result, e.g. the exam result you want, holding your degree certificate, relaxing in your newly refurbished home, driving to and from your great new job or living happily with your lovely partner.

It is common to spend time daydreaming instead of telling yourself what you want. When you command yourself to do things, you will do them.

Some things are tough to do, such as getting a university degree, but focus on the benefits of sticking with it and on the rewards you will gain from achieving it. Bringing up children can be challenging, but again, focus on the good things that will come from doing a great job and enjoy each stage of their upbringing. Work may be challenging, but the reward is knowing that you are doing a good job and contributing something of value to the world.

Everything you are doing is just a phase of your life. Enjoy the phase. See everything you do as a new learning experience towards developing your life experience and your skill set.

Kick boxer confidence technique

Pretend to be a kick boxer. Stand up and do the actions of a kick boxer – within your own fitness capabilities, of course! As you do the kick-boxing actions, boxing with your hands and kicking with your leg, say positive statements about what you want to achieve.

- 'I can do this. I am doing this. This is done.'

- 'I am doing it. I am doing it. I am doing it.'

- Add your own name to the beginning of the sentence: '[Your name], I am doing this.'

You will feel a positive energy running through your body as you do this exercise, helping you to believe that you can do whatever you need to get done. Your body has a muscle memory pattern and this will train it to feel the positive feelings that enable you to believe in yourself on every level.

Repeat the exercise regularly whenever you need to believe in yourself. For example, whenever you have studying or paperwork to do, say '[Your name], I can do it. I am doing it. It is done.' At any time when you are thinking otherwise, remind yourself to focus again.

People tend to self-sabotage by having negative

conversations with themselves. Here are some examples of positive things to say instead.

A student may say, 'I can learn this information. I am learning it. I am remembering it. It is done. I am doing AMAZINGLY well in my exams. I am an AMAZING student.'

A mother may say, 'I can get the kids into bed quickly and easily. I am doing it. It is done. My kids are sleeping through the night. I am relaxed about the kids.'

Someone in a challenging job may say, 'I can get this work done. I am doing it. It is done. The clients are happy. The staff are supportive. Everything is AMAZING.'

Someone looking for love may say, 'I can have a great partner. I am happily married. I am in a loving relationship. I am happy in myself and with my partner. I have a successful marriage. It is done.'

Someone looking for a better home may say, 'I can have an AMAZING home. I am living in an AMAZING home within budget, which is AMAZING for me. It is done.'

Someone in debt may say, 'I can clear my debt. I am clearing my debt. It is done. I am earning plenty of money. I am saving my money.'

Someone with health issues may say, 'I can be strong and fit. I am strong and fit. I have found all the solutions available to me to improve my health. I am well. I am looking after myself. I am healthy.'

You may not see all the results you want immediately, but your general conversation with yourself will be improving your positivity, and the more positive you become, the more positive your life will become. It's okay to have a negative moment, but quickly try to remind yourself to be positive again. Sometimes a negative feeling is our instinct trying to tell us to avoid something or to make another choice. So get in tune with your instinct too. Decide what the negative thinking or worry is and how your instinct may be trying to steer you in the right direction. Always assume things will work out AMAZINGLY well and your mind will help you to make good things happen. Sometimes, you will feel a knowing feeling that something needs to be done, so go with that feeling, as long as it is safe and positive.

By accepting where you are in life, regularly stating the outcome you want and actioning what you need to do to change things, you will make that outcome happen. We are, in effect, hypnotizing ourselves with the words we speak to ourselves and to other people. Remember that your words create your life. I have tried and tested this theory many times for myself. In the past, in situations when it was easy to think something was impossible, I found that self-talking myself into the positive made things happen very quickly.

As a hypnotherapist, I understand that the mind does what we tell it to do. But most of the time people are giving themselves mixed messages by using confused self-talk. Lots of people think they are attracting things from an outside source, whereas in fact it is the inner self-talk that is making the outside things happen. People often give away their power to outside influences. But everything is being created by you and how you deal with life. A successful businessman or businesswoman would not fall at the first hurdle. If something doesn't work out, they don't doubt themselves or their abilities. They find a way to make it happen, just as an athlete would do. Successful people have an inner belief and a drive that gives them a 'can-do, go-for-it' attitude. They are generally positive people who like to be around other positive, like-minded people who have a similar positive outlook.

We all tend to surround ourselves in life with people who are on a wavelength that is similar to ours. So, if it doesn't feel right being around negative people, you are probably ready to move up the positive scale and be with people who think like you do. It feels good to be around people you feel comfortable with. It feels like being with yourself when you are around the right people for you. As you improve your 'I can' outlook, you will notice that you begin to move in more positive circles of friends, family and colleagues. It's okay to let go of some of the people you know so that they can find the right people for them as you find the right people for you.

With this in mind, begin to do one thing from your list of things to get done. This will break the 'not doing' habit and begin to create a 'habit of doing' in your mind. The chances are that if you start with one thing, you'll go on to do two or three, even four or five, and will probably finish the whole list.

Remember all the times you have finished tasks or achieved goals in your daily life or at work. By reminding yourself of these achievements, you will begin to see that you are getting on with things all the time. The one thing you want to achieve now is just as easy as all the other things you have achieved without even thinking about them.

So, DO ONE THING.

If you are struggling to get started with one thing, take some deep breaths in and out and channel all your thoughts into the action of doing the task. As you are breathing in and out, say to yourself in your head, 'I can do this. I am doing this. It is done.' Even if the first thing you do is just move some papers, turn on the computer, open one email or make one decision, you have already begun the process of action.

- Begin with the easiest thing to get yourself started.

- When we action things, things get done.

- When we are in a positive frame of mind, more positive things happen.

Inner coach technique

Think of someone you admire who does the sort of thing you are trying to achieve. Imagine they are your coach and that they believe in you. What would they say to you? How would they encourage you? What advice would they give you?

Imagine they say AMAZING things to you. What would those things be?

For example, to someone who is redesigning their home, the coach may say: 'You have AMAZING style and creative ability. You are great with colours. You are fantastic at choosing interior decorations. You are clever at achieving professional results within a budget.'

To someone who is trying to get a new job, the coach may say: 'You have so many skills. Look at how good you are in your field of work. You have so much experience. You are an excellent candidate. I would definitely employ you.'

To someone who is looking for love, the coach may say: 'You are such a brilliant person. There are millions of people in the world and there are many AMAZING people out there for you. You will find someone special who totally adores you. You look gorgeous/handsome. You have an AMAZING personality. You are so kind. You are a great catch.'

To someone who wants to pay off their debts, the coach may say: 'You are talented and skilled and you can use those traits to find positive ways to pay off your debts. You are intelligent. You will find ways to take control of your finances. You will start saving so that you can make yourself financially secure. You will turn your finances around by being sensible with your money from now on. You can easily earn more money.'

To someone who wants to move to another home, the coach may say: 'There are millions of great properties out there and you are going to find an AMAZING one. You have all the skills to make good things happen for yourself.'

To someone who is studying, the coach may say: 'Look at what you have achieved so far. It is because you are AMAZING that you are even in this position to sit for these exams. You have AMAZING talent. You are going to focus on your studies and stick to a sensible time plan. You will remember the information. You are going to be delighted with the results. You are going to feel calm in your exams and you are going to do AMAZINGLY well.'

To someone who wants to lose weight or reduce their alcohol intake, the coach may say: 'You can let go. You can eat and drink sensibly. I have seen you do this many times. You are really good at making changes. You are really successful when you focus. I believe in you.'

Positive talk

The coach would not say anything insulting or negative, like the things many people say to themselves. It may take some time to get used to being your own positive coach in your head, as you may not be used to hearing positives about yourself. If you notice that the old voice is back, remember to switch to your positive voice again. Try to strengthen the positivity of every statement with even more positive words. Make the coach's enthusiasm really over the top. SMILE as you lap up the compliments. Get used to being praised by yourself.

- Even if you just do this technique once, you will have unlocked your mind so that it can climb out of the negative rut.

I have helped many clients with these techniques. I know that anyone can change, because, as a therapist, I see people do it on a daily basis. By changing the conversation in your head, you can achieve your goals.

I taught these techniques to a friend who plays golf. (He said he plays quite badly most of the time!) Instead of saying, 'I hope the ball doesn't go in the rough,' I told him to say to himself, 'I can get the ball into the hole. The ball is going into the hole.' A few weeks later, he told me that he had tried the technique when he was teeing off, saying to himself, 'Ball up. The ball is going up. The ball is going high up.' He kept repeating it and then hit the ball high up in the air, in a way he had never done before. The ball hit the roof of the practice range in which he was standing and bounced back, hitting him on the head and nearly knocking him out!

I told him, 'It's not the best idea to tell your mind to hit the ball up high when you are standing in a building with a roof! And, anyway, I thought you were going to try to get the ball in the hole.'

'I forgot,' he said.

'Well, try it next time,' I suggested.

But he said he was a bit frightened to try it again as the technique was so powerful, and we both laughed. It's worth noting, though, that it's always a good idea to be careful about what you are telling yourself to do.

Cut the Crap and Feel AMAZING is the first book I have written and there were a few moments, particularly when I started writing it, when self-doubt crept in. So I wrote this 'I can do it' motivation chapter first, then used the techniques I was describing to motivate myself. I also thought about all the hypnotherapy scripts I have written for my recordings and all the knowledge I have gained over the last few years, then self-talked myself into believing I could do it. Ten weeks later, I had written the whole book, and a few weeks after that, it was ready for printing.

Do something right NOW on your list of 'things to do' with this 'I can' attitude. Trust me: it will be AMAZING. I would love to see photographs of what you have achieved with your 'I can do it' attitude. So, please do send them to my Ailsa Frank blog, Twitter @AilsaFrank or Instagram ailsafrank

Cut the self-doubt from your life and feel AMAZING.

Chapter summary

✂ 'I can do it. I am doing it. It is done.'

✂ Don't just see things as being either black or white. Remember that the grey area has all the solutions. There are many ways of doing things or resolving things. So look for answers.

✂ Give things a try. You don't need to be 100% ready – 90% is good enough.

✂ Use the teacher technique: tell yourself you will do it and listen to yourself as you would listen to a teacher.

✂ Use the feeling satisfied technique: feel the feeling of being satisfied and relieved that the things you want to achieve are already done before you begin them.

✂ Each stage of your life is a phase. Enjoy every phase by relaxing into everyday life.

✂ Use the kick boxer technique: stand up and do the actions of a kick boxer as you speak out loud what you want to achieve. Say, 'I can do it. I am doing it. It is done.'

✄ Present yourself well. Dress appropriately. Exude a confident posture.

✄ When good things happen, make a 'snapshot in your mind' and bank it in your AMAZING zone.

✄ Start with one task. Pick the easiest thing to do to get you started and before you know it you'll have finished what you needed to get done.

✄ Use the inner coach technique: imagine you are an expert in what you are trying to achieve, then self-talk yourself to be successful. What would a coach say to encourage you?

STEP 1. Set a goal.

STEP 2. Think AMAZING.

STEP 3. Make it happen.

In this age of information sharing, everyone can access the knowledge they need to become successful if they look for the answers.

CHAPTER 6

MONEY AND
WEALTH

This is one of the most important chapters in the book because money is at the root of your life. Every choice and decision you make revolves around how much money you have, which affects everything from what you can buy in the supermarket to where you are able to live. In my experience, many people say, 'I don't need more money,' or 'I haven't got a problem with money,' and then go on to tell me a hundred and one problems that are, in fact, all related to money.

It is not just how much money you have that's important. What also matters is how you feel about the money you have. Many people don't realize they are wealthy until they lose their wealth or become financially worse off. So, today, begin to feel contented with what you already have and start building on this.

- Anyone can become rich or poor.

- A lower-income steady saver can end up wealthier than a high-flying risk-taker.

There are people from the poorest and the richest backgrounds who become successful and who experience being stressed or frustrated about money. So let go of the past and try to stop comparing yourself to other people, worrying about where you came from or what you did or didn't have. It really is your choice whether you are inspired or disheartened about your ability to create a secure financial life. Start to feel good about money from now onwards.

By letting go of the negative beliefs and using the AMAZING and SMILE techniques combined with good choices and decisions, you can begin to carve out the financial life you want. Start to love your finances. Feel great about money. When you feel positive about money, you will make better money decisions. If you are frustrated by money, money will frustrate you. But if you love your finances, you will become someone who has finances to love.

Anyone can shop in any of the different types of supermarkets. Some people shop more in the expensive ones, while others shop in the cheaper ones. It doesn't matter how rich or poor you are, by making clever decisions and choices you can shop in all of them on your budget. Buy a small treat in a more expensive shop, even if you can only afford to do it once a year, and buy everyday things in the more budget-conscious shops. You don't need to wait until you can afford to do all your shopping all the time in the expensive supermarket. By realizing that you can afford to have the experience of wealth as long as you stick to your budget and balance your spending, you can feel well off immediately.

You can apply the supermarket concept to every aspect of your life and feel wealthy straight away, rather than waiting to be wealthy. If you can't afford your own jet right now, you might be able to save up enough money to have one flying lesson! Start being creative about how you can begin to live the life you would ideally have. But always stick to your budget. When you believe your desires are possible, they begin to become reality. Someone may even invite you to go on their jet, so don't assume you have to own a jet to go on one.

- Budgeting = you spend less money than you receive so that you can save too.

The important thing is to accept what you have now – 'This is where I am' – and feel good about it. SMILE and laugh as if your finances are AMAZING. If they are not AMAZING right now, you will start to laugh about them rather than feeling stressed by them. If your finances are already AMAZING but you want to improve them further, these suggestions will also help you.

From now onwards, feel good about money. Make the most of your choices and decisions to use your money wisely and earn income in the best way you can. Unexpected amounts of money may come to you, but you need to be practical and get that better-paid job too. There is no point saying an affirmation such as, 'Unexpected huge sums of money come to me regularly,' 300 times a day. It is limiting to fill your head with one thought so many times a day. Instead, have a practical, positive general self-talk about whatever is most relevant to you.

- 'I have an AMAZING job that I love and that suits me.'
- 'I have AMAZING money in my life.'
- 'I have finances that make me SMILE.'
- 'I have spare money to invest.'
- 'I have plenty of money in the bank.'
- 'I am clever with my money.'
- 'I have financial security.'
- 'I earn plenty of money.'
- 'I am good at earning money.'
- 'I pay my bills easily.'

Keep your thoughts positive and varied, like a radio station playing in your head. If you hear negative thoughts creeping in, remember to tune back in to the positive radio station again.

A person doing a highly paid job and working long hours

may end up being no better off financially than a lower-paid person, because they spend everything they earn on rewarding themselves for the hard work they do. They may overstretch themselves by buying expensive items, eating out or ordering takeaways because they haven't got time to cook, paying for school fees and expensive holidays, and buying a big house they can't afford. Eventually, they may be even more stressed about money than someone on a lower wage who is living within their budget.

Over the years, I have had many clients who were burned out from working long hours and paying large sums of money to commute to London, which was also having an impact on their quality of life. People can feel trapped in their jobs and by financial commitments. They can be so caught up in the life they have created that they can't see any way to get out of it. Through the work I do with these clients, I help them to see that there is always a way to change what you are doing by gradually making different choices and decisions and by starting to feel better in your daily routine.

You can feel stressed on your journey to work or you can feel relaxed and enjoy the time, seeing it as quality time for yourself. Once you start to say to yourself, 'AMAZING things are happening,' and use the SMILE technique, you will identify the things that don't work for you so that you can start to adjust your life in subtle ways.

Many of my clients have gone on to change their jobs, taking lower-paid local jobs that allow them to finish their working day earlier so that they have time to do the things they want to do, like cooking, reading or doing other hobbies. They generally feel more relaxed and have more time to work out ways of saving money so that they can live comfortably on their reduced budget. And they end up being financially better off, have more time to themselves and are under less pressure at work, which are all positive life changes.

Other clients use my techniques to learn ways to manage their stress better and then discover that their new, more positive attitude brings better, more financially rewarding opportunities into their lives. By starting to view things differently, they begin to make better choices and create the life they were striving for in the first place. Others go on to retrain and get better jobs, streamline their businesses or climb the career ladder with a more positive attitude, which helps them deal with work in a more relaxed way.

Your biggest asset is yourself – how you earn your money, how you use your money and how you choose to live your life. Quality of life is the key to happiness. Although money is important, there is no point earning vast sums of it if you don't feel good about your life.

People often decide on a career without thinking about how doing that particular job will make them feel each day, or what the routine will actually be. Some people choose a job because of the money they will be paid, while some don't even think about how much they will earn. The answer is to use your skills in the best way for you, make the choices that are best for you, and create the life you love.

There is no point having a gorgeous, expensive car if you are driving it every day to a job you hate. Rather than burden yourself with expenses you can't really afford, it is more satisfying to drive a car that doesn't overstretch your finances and then perhaps hire a Ferrari occasionally for a day. This will be much cheaper than actually owning an expensive car.

- Think before you spend. If you have a bad feeling about buying something, don't spend the money.

The following exercise will help you to get your mind out of your current rigid thinking, which may be limiting your success with money.

The dough technique

Making money and being successful result from a series of processes, which are similar to the processes involved in making bread. This technique will help you to expand your mind and have a wealthy life, using the bread-making process.

To build your wealth you need to plan, be organized, do all the different parts of the process – such as buy, sell and invest – at the right time to make money, exert physical effort and then allow time for things to mature and expand before you are eventually able to enjoy the results of your efforts. Think of your finances while you imagine the process of making bread – the weighing of the ingredients, the mixing of the ingredients, the kneading of the dough, the rising of the bread and the baking in the oven. The growth of your finances will also develop from a similar series of events and processes.

Imagine kneading a ball of dough, moving it, stretching it in different directions, getting rid of the lumps and making it smooth. You can move your hands as you do it. As you imagine the relaxing feeling of kneading the dough, think about your finances, feel the feeling of working through things and sorting them out so that you can progress to the next level of wealth.

Imagine your financial plans working out well. As you feel these feelings, imagine that your mind is becoming solution-focused and that you are thinking in the best possible way so that your finances will be easy, flowing and smooth like the dough.

Imagine some things taking care of themselves, just as the dough rises on its own and the oven bakes the bread. Imagine many good things happening in your life. You automatically make good decisions and while certain things take care of themselves, you take action to deal with the others.

As you think about kneading the dough, imagine being in the right place at the right time for good things to happen. Imagine that wonderful things are possible for you. Imagine that things are working out well.

Now imagine creatively turning the dough into bread shapes. Choose a shape in your mind, perhaps a baguette or bread rolls or a loaf of bread. Choose whatever feels right for you. You might choose a different shape each time you do this exercise. You can move your hands as if you are making the bread shape you have chosen.

When you are ready, allow the dough to rise and feel satisfied with your bread shape, with your financial shape and with your finances. Imagine everything working out well. Imagine popping the bread into the oven and the oven baking the bread. Imagine your finances progressing to the next level, just as the bread reaches its final stage of cooking.

Imagine that you have done everything today and each day to progress your wealth to the next stage. Each day you do what needs to be done for your finances to grow. Just as the baker makes the bread every day, you make a daily contribution to your wealth. You create financial security and a wealthy, happy lifestyle. SMILE as you feel good about your finances.

Repeat this exercise regularly. Remember it any time you think of your finances. Remember things are working out well as you work through each stage to build your finances. You are gradually working through things, bit by bit, and making sensible choices. Just as the bread rises up, you will rise to the next level of financial security and wealth. Think of the kneading of the dough as being you working through the problems to create solutions, kneading your career, your finances…

Be in control of your finances and feel AMAZING.

Chapter summary

✂ Talk positively to yourself about money.

✂ Plan your financial future.

✂ Say 'AMAZING money' and SMILE.

✂ Use the dough technique: imagine working through your finances just as you would knead a ball of dough. Allow your finances to mature in the same way as a baker makes a loaf of bread.

✂ Love your finances as much as you love being snuggled up in a cosy bed.

STEP 1. Enjoy what you already have.

STEP 2. Live life within your budget.

STEP 3. Work at improving your financial future.

You got into debt through a series of choices and decisions. You will get out of it by making new choices and decisions.

CHAPTER 7

DEBT

Cut the debt from your life and feel AMAZING

There are several types of debt:

- Debt due to overspending – buying things you can't afford.

- Debt to survive – being on a very low income.

- Debt resulting from a change of circumstances – due to being made redundant, loss of income or wealth, illness, bereavement, divorce.

- Debt that is an investment, such as a mortgage or a student loan.

Whichever type of debt you have, you need to look at why you have it and where you can cut back on spending, as every small saving will help towards you becoming financially stable and paying off your loans. It may have taken some time to get into debt, so you may need to spend some time getting out of it. During that time, AMAZING, unexpected things can happen too. So be optimistic as well as realistic. You can work your way out of any situation, and that is what you need to focus on.

Look at every single thing you are spending your money on. Most people can cut back even more than they think they can. For instance, a client told me, 'My food shopping is so expensive I have cut back to the bare minimum. But it still costs me a fortune.' After a discussion, she disclosed that she was buying chicken breasts wrapped in Parma ham, which she served with fresh pasta for her family of five. To me, that would be something you served at a dinner party, not as a midweek family meal. But in her mind it was normal. Although that would be fine for someone who could afford it, for my client it was taking money she didn't have out of her tight budget. Her lavish food shopping was preventing her from being able to save money and have financial security.

Some of your expenses are hidden, so really look at the price of everything you pick up before you buy it and check for cheaper alternatives. A whole chicken works out at half the price of chicken breasts. And what is the point of eating chicken breasts if you have credit-card debts that stop you sleeping at night?

Start clearing your debts immediately, even if you just pay £1 towards them. It may take you a year or two to pay them off, but first you have to create the habit of doing it. Start to get yourself into the habit of being in control of your finances. Then, once you have cleared your debts and have got into the habit of putting money aside, you can carry on being careful with your money, build up savings and secure your financial future. Don't build a financial future based on repeating old, bad habits and racking up more debt.

You are likely to have inherited your money habits from your upbringing. Try to identify where your bad money habits came from so that you can rectify your behaviour. When you were a child, did your household yo-yo between famine and feast? Were you aware of your parents being in debt? Did your parents buy now and pay later? Were you handed money with no explanation of its value? Did you get what you wanted as a child, so expect to have everything you want now? Did your parents have a lot of money and you are struggling to replicate the lifestyle you were used to as a child?

- Did your past cast a negative spell over your financial life?

- Were you aware of your parents' spending and now want to avoid some of the pitfalls they experienced?

- What can you improve on?

Happiness is being contented with what you have

You may like to have good meals out, drive a nice car, buy new clothes and go on luxury holidays, but if you can't afford it, then you *really* can't afford it. You have to accept this. It might be hard to hear, but if you don't accept it, your spending will eventually catch up with you. Your finances are your responsibility, not the government's, not a family member's. And your financial problems are yours and yours alone. If you have children, they are also your responsibility until they are grown-up, whether you live with them or not. Don't expect other people to pay for your financial decisions. You need to take responsibility for yourself and for your family. If you made bad choices in the past, you need to understand what they were so that you can avoid making them again and make better choices from now onwards. Always believe in AMAZING solutions and in things working out well.

I have seen many people lose their homes due to living beyond their wealth and refusing to do without the things they believe to be 'essential'. Instead of changing their spending or improving their circumstances, they simply build up more debt. Once someone has lost their home, it is often easy for them to look back and see how out of balance their spending was and that they bought things they couldn't afford because they wouldn't accept their situation. But some people won't change until it is too late. Many people don't want to hear from a friend or a wife or husband that they can't afford the lifestyle they want.

Try to listen to what other people who are financially secure have to say, as they may have some answers for you.

Some people believe the universe will provide for them. But some fail to combine this with a business head and a plan of action. People can live on the edge of financial crisis, expecting to live off miracles instead of being practical about creating their wealth. Miracles do happen, so enjoy them when they do. But keep your feet on the ground in the real world too.

A client who had some debt and who had set up a new online shop decided to buy a bigger car because her instinct told her she was going to need it to take all the parcel deliveries to the post office. In reality, there was a lot of competition for her type of business, which made it difficult to attract visitors to her website and she only had a few orders a week. She was selling items that were quite small and that she could easily have carried to the post box in her handbag. She certainly didn't need a large new car for deliveries. It would have been better for her to have visualized and aspired to having a business that would one day justify a delivery vehicle. Sometimes, it is easy to become so wrapped up in something that you don't see the reality. A good businessperson would have kept their expenses low until the business justified further investment.

- All the guidance in the world won't help if you don't combine it with common sense.

I have helped many clients turn their finances around through positive thinking and practical action. There is nothing you need to own that it is worth risking your security to buy.

- Stop buying things you can't afford.

- If you can't afford to buy even reduced/sale items, you have to accept it.

- Stop playing catch-up. You are gambling with your future.

- Remember things you can't afford to buy today will cause you stress tomorrow.

- Get all the financial support and advice you can.

- Compare yourself to people who have less. That way you will feel wealthier.

- If you constantly aspire, you will never pause long enough to appreciate the wealth you already have.

- Downsize everything to get back in control.

- Find free ways to enjoy your life – go for a walk or a run, read a book, have a picnic in the park.

- Be happy for other people's good fortune. Be inspired, not jealous.

- Feel great about the money you do have. Feel AMAZING and SMILE.

- Say, 'It would be nice to have those things,' rather than needing them.

- Pay off your debt. Don't be in a situation where you have negative people chasing after you.

- Use your skills. Build your skills.

- Secure a good foundation of wealth before you try to climb the wealth ladder.

- Every money choice and decision is shaping your future. Think before you purchase.

- If you are self-employed, put your tax money away as you receive payments.

Don't gamble with your future

Re-evaluate what is essential and re-evaluate how best to use your time. For example, only free TV channels are 'essential'. Don't watch daytime TV. Instead, stick to a working day, get up early and be proactive to source a job or invest your time retraining. Use your evenings wisely, searching for better-paid work or making a plan of how to change your spending. People often pin their hopes on winning the lottery, which is simply a form of gambling. Instead, take control of your life. Retraining takes time but is a good investment of your time. Improving your skills will make a real difference to your finances, as your job will probably be your biggest source of income. Making the excuse that it will take too long to retrain will only prolong the time you spend in the poverty state. If you have a good job already, make a point each day of feeling good about it. Feel proud of what you have achieved so far.

Risking money by gambling to earn money is just a way of avoiding facing the fact that you need to change yourself and your behaviour towards work, career, money and savings. I have had many clients over the years who were gambling money they didn't have, running up debts behind their spouses' back, risking the security of their families and future for what they believed was a quick fix and a fast route to getting rich. Gambling rarely pays off, whereas making better choices and decisions works every time.

Be careful about investing the money of friends or family in a venture, and be cautious about trading in stocks and shares. You need to weigh up the risks, because it could all go wrong.

Crisis

Sometimes, people are plummeted into a financial crisis for reasons beyond their control, such as bereavement, divorce or health issues. Try to believe that things will work out AMAZINGLY well. Use letting-go techniques, such as the red triangle technique described in Chapter 3, to offload stress. Imagine putting your worries into a red triangle in your mind and visualize it shrinking down and dissolving. You can also use the technique of rubbing, pressing or tapping your left knuckles while saying 'Let it pass' and seeing the worries in your mind pass by like clouds in the sky. If you are ill, do whatever you can to get well as quickly as possible. Know that you will find a way through things. There may be a way to bring in some income, so be open to this possibility. If you are claiming benefits, work towards a bigger picture of becoming self-supporting.

The more positive you are, the better. Keep a positive feeling by self-coaching: 'I can do this. I am doing this. It is done. I can turn this into a positive. I can work through this. I can get over this.' Keep your mind in the AMAZING zone. Say, 'It will work out AMAZINGLY well.' This may sound strange when you have a real crisis to deal with. But by keeping the AMAZING feeling going, you will ensure that your mind doesn't slip into negative thinking and you will come up with the best solutions sooner. Through good choices and decisions, you will start to turn things around. When you are focused on the 'AMAZING' happening, AMAZING things will come your way. I am not saying that you will win the lottery (although you may!), but opportunities will come your way or extra money from various sources, or maybe you'll find some health solutions so that you can get back to work, or a bereavement could open new doors of opportunity for you.

Just as your circumstances became bad as the result of a series of events, it is a series of events that will make your situation good again. Always imagine that there is an AMAZING way through things and you will be pleasantly surprised. If someone has taken your wealth from you, do what you can to get it back, but don't waste your time on negative past situations. Instead, keep positively moving forwards. Negative people from your past are part of the past problem and you may never win with them. Feel good about what has happened, learn from it, analyse what you could have done differently and feel that it will work out AMAZINGLY well, focus on the future not on the past. As you build new wealth moving forwards, make sure that, this time, you look after it.

Make a plan of action

Don't just believe that AMAZING things happen. Take action and do what needs to be done to improve the situation.

Action changing your wealth. When money comes your way, don't think, 'Oh good, I can go out now.' Instead, use the extra money to pay off debt to enable you to have the life you want.

One client, who was in a terrible financial situation, received some extra money for some work she had done and told me, 'It's a sign that I can have my nails done.' She was wrong! Just because she was thinking about not being able to have her nails done, the money didn't appear so that she could pay for it. Your priority needs to be to pay to keep a roof over your head, not for things that aren't essential or for other people to do things that you could actually do yourself. It was at that moment that I knew why my client was always in debt: her priority was luxuries, not securing financial stability.

It is a program in the subconscious mind that makes it seem normal to spend when you don't have money to spare. You need to retrain your mind to secure your financial position by identifying the problems and then making different choices. Hypnotherapy is a quick way to reprogram the subconscious part of your mind. I believe that listening regularly to wealth-related hypnosis recordings will release and override a lifetime of bad money habits.

Insane money thinking

Buying a big car or buying or renting a large property you can't afford and then hoping the money will be there to pay for it is insane. It is a good idea to research things you are not ready to buy but when you make the purchase make sure you are in a good financial position to afford it.

I would suggest that you buy the smallest, newest car you can afford or rent the cheapest reasonable home, which may mean downsizing so that you can take control of your finances. If you are buying a property, be realistic about what you can afford.

The following are some 'insanity money' stories to make you think about what you might be doing that you could change.

1. A client called Sue told me that she and her husband were working very hard but could afford little in the way of luxuries or holidays. She was comparing herself to her friend Katie. Katie was a 'stay-at-home mum' whose husband had a job that wasn't especially well paid but the family had two luxury holidays a year, ate meals out regularly, bought lots of new clothes and expensive new cars. My client, Sue, said, 'It's so unfair. What are we doing wrong?'

   'You don't know your friend's true circumstances,' I told her. 'As you said yourself, you need to earn a lot of money to have that sort of lifestyle. Most people can't afford it. Maybe Katie and her husband have an inheritance, or maybe they have run up credit-card debts to pay for the way they live.'

   A month later, at her next appointment, Sue said, 'You were right. My friend and her husband are in terrible debt. They have just put their house on the market.'

My advice: Don't make assumptions about other people's wealth, because you don't have all the facts. Instead, focus on your own wealth and your financial facts by making AMAZING choices and decisions for you. If you lose your house for some reason, make sure you rent something cheaper so that you can save to get yourself back on the property ladder again.

2. Tom decided he wanted to buy a large new car and took out a loan, repayable at £600 per month over 5 years. His wife disagreed with his decision, as she was quite happy to continue to share the car they already had.

My advice: People often think taxis are expensive, but when you add up all the expenses of buying and running a second vehicle, it may be cheaper to use taxis quite regularly. Buy the smallest, cheapest, newest car you can easily afford. Think of the feelings that will result from the decision you make. How will you feel making the monthly payments when the car is getting old and has depreciated in value?

3. Eric had spent his life up to the age of 55 spending money and saying, 'It's only £20 or £50 or £100. It isn't going to change my lifestyle.' He came from a wealthy background and was constantly trying to keep up with the lifestyle he had been used to. Eventually, all the little overspends cost him his home and everything in it. Years of remortgaging and building up overdrafts had finally caught up with him. At one stage, he could have downsized, sold his house and bought a smaller one mortgage-free so that he could pay off his debts. But he and his wife wouldn't let go of the big house and have to admit to their friends that they couldn't afford their lifestyle. In the end, his lifestyle

changed so much that he often ate the food other people had left on their plates in cafés.

My advice: Every single choice you make has a consequence. So use your money wisely and secure yourself financially.

4. James and his wife had children at university but spent all their savings on furniture, a new kitchen and bathroom. James did not agree with his wife's decision to renovate their house, which put them under pressure and caused a lot of tension in their relationship. James was worried about the money, which they couldn't afford to spend, particularly as they were helping their children financially while they were at university.

My advice: Create security and don't leave yourself vulnerable by overcommitting financially. Renovate your home on a budget – a fresh coat of paint and some new taps in the bathroom rather than a complete makeover. You can have the AMAZING kitchen when you have security and money to spare. If you are in a relationship, you need to make joint decisions that make sense financially.

5. Rebecca invested in too many properties, which she rented out. When the recession hit, the rent she was getting wasn't enough to cover all the mortgage repayments. This caused her a lot of stress because the properties were worth less than she had paid for them, so she couldn't sell them.

My advice: Make manageable investments. Sometimes, people get too deep into financial commitments that push them into bankruptcy. Don't overstretch yourself with investments you won't be able to afford if circumstances change. Make AMAZING choices and decisions to build a secure financial future.

6. Diane and her husband sold their house to free up more money to live off and to be mortgage-free. They didn't want the responsibility of a mortgage, but once they had moved into a rented place, they realized that the rent had to be paid every month, just like the mortgage had been. Also, they would have to pay the rent forever, even in retirement, when they would have less income.

My advice: Rent out your home and find a cheaper rental property to live in if you don't want to pay a mortgage, or get a lodger to help you pay it. But remember that as you get older, you may not be able to get a mortgage again. So think carefully before you get rid of it. A property you own is likely – although not guaranteed – to increase in value, giving you more options of where to live later if you have some equity in it.

Think 'AMAZING' so that you are in the right place at the right time for a good property deal. When you are in the AMAZING zone, you may even be offered somewhere to live for free!

7. Tracey, a self-employed, married working mum who I was helping with her finances, was feeling pressurized by her lack of money. There was never any money left each month to do anything other than pay all the essential bills. Tracey *really* wanted to redecorate the lounge and get rid of the old, stained carpet. I suggested throwing away the carpet, painting the old floor boards and buying a couple of cheap rugs and some scatter cushions for the couch.

When I saw Tracey again two months later, I asked her how the painted floor was looking. She told me she was stressed about not having the money to pay her tax bill because, after discussing the painted floor idea with friends, she had decided to spend £2000 on having a new wooden floor laid in the lounge. Her friends had put her off the idea of painting the existing floor, saying that it would get damaged. (In fact, any damage could easily be touched up with more paint.)

So the good feeling of having the new wooden floor had, in fact, been wiped out by the stress caused by spending her tax money. A painted floor would have given her the makeover she wanted in the lounge, left her plenty of money to pay her tax and allowed her to save a bit towards the cost of a new floor, which she could have had in a couple of years' time. Now, every time she looks at the floor, she feels bad about the overspend. She told me later that it was a big lesson for her and that she is now careful to put tax money to one side and accept that she has to save up if she wants to buy something, rather than put herself under financial pressure.

My advice: If you can't afford it today, how are you going to pay for it tomorrow? Think before you spend. Be creative about achieving things on a budget. Your tax money is not yours to spend. Remember this story and try to break bad habits of overspending. When you receive payments for work done, put 20–30% of it away in a special tax savings account – and any VAT into another account. It is a good idea also to put money away for Christmas and birthday presents so that you are in control of your finances.

Work at changing your finances

If you imagine a big wheel that has been turning in the wrong direction as you were overspending and getting caught up in debt, you now have to turn the cog so that the wheel goes the other way. To start with, that can involve some strain and effort. But if you remain focused on getting out of debt and making yourself financially secure, eventually the cog will move easily and you'll be back on track with everything.

You created the problem, so you will get yourself out of it too – as long as you stop burying your head in the sand.

Cut the debt from your life and feel AMAZING.

Chapter summary

✂ Change your behaviour towards money.

✂ Make plans to reduce debt. Set up a debt payment plan.

✂ Get yourself financially secure as quickly as possible.

✂ Start saving regularly, even if it is only £1 at a time.

✂ Learn from people who are good with money.

STEP 1. Reduce spending.

STEP 2. Clear debt.

STEP 3. Be sensible with your money.

It is possible for anyone to become wealthier.

CHAPTER 8

AMAZING
MONEY STORIES

Budget for the occasional affordable treat that will make you feel wealthy. You may only be able to afford to do this once a month or once a year. But look forward to it, enjoy it while you are doing it and feel great about it after the event. When you are enjoying an event, take a 'snapshot in your mind' of the happiness so that you can remember the feeling of the enjoyment any time you think about it in the future. A good memory can be as enjoyable as actually being there. Bank the AMAZING feeling to enhance your AMAZING zone. It could be the enjoyment you feel when having a meal out, a boat trip or a visit to an expensive jewellery shop where you don't buy anything but have a coffee at the fancy café next door.

Start living as if you are wealthy – within your budget – and believe in great things. Always keep money in your wallet, but train yourself not to spend it. If you don't have spare cash to do this, put some pieces of paper in your wallet so that it feels as if it's overflowing. When you feel good about money, AMAZING things will happen to you.

Re-address your spending

Catherine, a 30-year-old professional woman who is one of my clients, told me she couldn't afford to buy a property. We discussed how much she spent on clothes, alcohol, going out, impulse purchases, magazines, unused hair and make-up products, and came to the conclusion that it amounted to a lot of wasted money. I then worked with her to change the negative spending habits in her mind.

Within a couple of months of making changes to her spending, Catherine had paid off some of her credit-card debts. Within a year, she had saved enough for a deposit and, by being realistic about the areas she could afford to buy in, was able to buy a property.

My advice: By looking at the financial facts, you can see where you are going wrong. Different choices and decisions will make your dreams come true.

Money can come from unexpected sources

A client called Trisha told me that she had to move to another part of the country temporarily, for six months, and didn't need her furniture at the new place. She was stressed because she didn't have the money to put her furniture into storage until she returned to the area and she couldn't leave it in the flat, which she was only renting. After working to release the negative stress, I told her to imagine the move had all worked out AMAZINGLY well and that it was financially AMAZING too. She was sceptical, but said she would give it a go.

Two weeks later, Trisha came back for another session and told me the most AMAZING story. A man who was a potential new tenant came to view the flat she was moving out of. As he was leaving, he popped his head back around the door and said, 'You wouldn't be interested in letting me rent your furniture for six months if I take the flat, would you?' So, on the day Trisha moved out, she packed her food, clothes and toiletries into her car and drove away. In exchange for being able to leave all her furniture and general household belongings in the flat, she was being paid £400 a month. Instead of having to pay storage fees, she had an income. Now, that is AMAZING!

My advice: Work to release the negative beliefs by following the techniques in this book and then presume things will work out AMAZINGLY well. If you do have to store your belongings have a good clear-out so you don't pay to store things you don't need.

AMAZING things can happen

A client called Nigel told me he couldn't continue struggling to pay all the costs of having children and general living expenses and that, as he only had enough money to pay the interest on his mortgage, the amount he owed was never going to reduce. After working in the session to release his negative fears, I told him, 'Things can happen. Things change. Think AMAZING.'

Less than a week later, Nigel's father-in-law decided to give his daughter and her husband £100,000 to reduce their mortgage. Nigel was AMAZED at how the AMAZING had worked!

My advice: You may not have a rich relative, but you don't need to know what the AMAZING, unexpected things will be. Just know that they *will* be AMAZING. Be open to paying off your mortgage early. Say to yourself, 'We've paid off the mortgage in an AMAZING way.'

Even a bad situation can turn into the best thing

A self-employed client lost his best customer, which meant that his income stopped almost overnight. I helped him to believe that it was AMAZING for him. A few days after his appointment with me, he woke up with the idea of pushing into other markets. The old client had made him so busy he had overlooked more lucrative areas of work. He kept the AMAZING feeling going, which led him to find new, better clients and to take his business in an AMAZING direction.

My advice: By releasing the negative beliefs and keeping in the AMAZING zone, you can make even better things happen.

Get the job you want with the salary you want

Sarah, a freelance journalist, was offered a dream job working for a magazine. But she didn't want to accept it because it involved a significant reduction in her salary. I did some hypnotherapy sessions with her and used some of the techniques described in this book to change her self-worth and financial value. I explained to her, 'It isn't your dream job unless you have the salary you want.'

You can make AMAZING things happen when you let go of old, limiting habits in your subconscious mind. After the session, Sarah's new confidence and positive self-belief enabled her to tell her prospective employer that she would only accept the job if the salary was the figure she wanted. The company agreed to pay her what she asked for. So she got her dream job and dream salary, and over the next couple of months she used the money that was still owed to her to clear her credit cards, putting her totally on top of her finances.

The AMAZING thing about this story is that the magazine that gave Sarah her dream job and salary was the same one that had originally commissioned her as a freelance journalist to write an article about how my hypnotherapy services could make her wealthier!

My advice: Think through how AMAZING you are and why you deserve a better salary. Then have the confidence to ask for it. Think AMAZING outcome. Say, 'I can do it. I am doing it. It is done. I have an AMAZING job and AMAZING salary.' If you don't get that job, your new positivity will already be creating an opportunity for something better to come your way.

Increase your sales

Mark was a salesman who had had a run of a few months with low sales. He began to feel bad about selling and found that he couldn't tell prospective customers about all the products because it sounded as though he was trying to get lots of money from them. So, to avoid the anxiety he felt when he told them about all the items in the range, he limited himself to mentioning just a few. After I worked to release the recent negative program that had built up in his mind, he felt relief. A few weeks later, he called to say that he had been responsible for the biggest sale the company had ever had!

My advice: If you are having a bad run of sales, be aware that it is just a habit that has developed in your subconscious mind and that can be easily rectified. You can use the letting-go techniques described in Chapter 3 and positive visualization: SMILE and say 'AMAZING'. Think of selling as informing the client of all the options. They will ultimately do what is right for them and knowing all the options available will be helpful to them. Hypnotherapy sessions and recordings are perfect for keeping in the positive sales zone. In fact, every salesperson I have ever worked with as a hypnotherapist has gone on to increase their sales figures.

Try hypnotherapy to increase your wealth

Sam bought my hypnotherapy recording *Money – Increase your Wealth*, which she listened to in order to help her change bad money beliefs and get out of a financial rut. After listening to it over a period of two months, she doubled her annual income from £18,000 to £36,000 because she had the confidence to apply for a much better-paid job and – to her surprise – she got it.

My advice: Be open to hypnotherapy.

Be your own boss

Steve, an experienced builder and senior executive in a building firm, had the idea of starting up a new building business but, due to the recession, he thought it might be too risky. After some appointments with me, he decided to leave his old job. Then, by using the AMAZING zone feeling, he self-talked himself into success and used other techniques described in this book to keep himself positive. He did some freelance work to help pay his bills before his own building projects were up and running. 'I had the self-belief to go after my dream despite the recession,' he told me. 'Because I had a new inner confidence, I packed in my job and have begun to create my own destiny.'

With hard work and believing in the AMAZING, his turnover in the first year was one million pounds! By the third year, he was turning over five million pounds.

My advice: Remember, Steve was starting a business with skills he had built up over many years, which is very different from starting a new business that you know nothing about. So, while you build a new business and new skills, be aware that you may need to keep doing your old job to support yourself until you start earning money. Being self-employed is hard work, so be prepared to put in the hours to set things up. Treat every customer with respect, as they could lead you to more customers. Keep expenses down, and be careful – it could be a while before you build up a good reputation and create a good income. Sometimes in life, you just have to go for things because they feel right. Your determination and good feelings will make you successful.

Focus determines your reality. Believe AMAZING things will happen, but be grounded too.

Sometimes you can have what you thought you couldn't afford

Gemma couldn't afford a holiday, so I worked with her to release her negative beliefs. I told her to imagine that it was the end of the summer and to feel as if she had had an AMAZING time. She was easily able to do this, as she was in a much more positive way of thinking after the session I did with her. A couple of weeks later, she told me that she had been offered a holiday home free of charge by a friend she hadn't seen for many years. So guess what: she had an AMAZING holiday after all.

My advice: AMAZING unexpected things do happen. Don't rely on them, but always feel filled with positive optimism. Releasing the negative beliefs is key to being positive on a subconscious level, which will allow you to really believe in good things happening instead of just pretending you feel positive.

Save, save, save, invest, invest, invest

Open several savings accounts and every time you earn or receive money, put some of it into each of them. When you think you don't have any spare money to save, cut back somewhere else so that you can put some into the savings accounts. This is very important psychologically, because when you think about your finances you will know that, as well as having debt or an overdraft, you also have some savings. By saving, you will program yourself to keep to a tighter budget and you will appreciate the things you are able to buy.

When I advised a client called Graham to do this, he said, 'I can't afford to save.' 'You can't afford not to save,' I told him. After I released his negative money patterns, despite having an overdraft, he decided to stretch himself and put £75 a month into a savings account. After 32 months, he had saved £2400. And when an expensive school trip came up for his daughter, which previously would have sent him into stress mode, he paid £200 from his current account and £600 from the savings account.

BEFORE he started saving, he said, 'It doesn't make sense because I pay more interest on my overdraft than the interest I gain on the savings.'

AFTER saving for 32 months, he said, 'It feels great knowing I have a buffer. It was a wise decision. Even though I pay the occasional overdraft fee, it has spurred me on to keep saving in the long term and to spend less so that I don't increase my overdraft. I've had a smaller overdraft since I started saving. It's hassle-free because I have a standing order to pay money from the bank into the savings account. So it's like paying any other bill. I was used to being "in overdraft", but now I am used to being "in savings" instead.'

To get out of overdraft you need to say, 'I have so much money in my accounts. My accounts are overflowing with money. I have plenty of savings.' This will break the negative thinking of the past ('I never have enough money').

I advise people to get rid of store loyalty cards, which tempt you into buying goods you don't need. Buy fresh, simple ingredients – meat, fish, eggs, dairy, nuts, pulses, fruit and vegetables – and cook your own food. You don't need packaged goods, so buy as few of them as possible. You also don't need lots of cleaning products, expensive Clingfilm and baking foil. Remember, a lot of goods are luxuries you can't afford. Think wartime and be careful with everything. You will be surprised by how much you already have in your cupboards. Be thrifty and create money by buying less. Every time you throw something away, ask yourself how much money it cost and be aware of how much you are wasting. Over the years, I have noticed that some of my wealthiest clients are the ones who quibble most over the cost of things. They are always looking for a bargain and a good investment. And they look after their money, which is probably one of the reasons why they became rich in the first place.

A really clever wealthy person is someone who creates quality of life too. There is no point working seven days a week, getting only four hours sleep a night, working away from home and living in airports and hotels, or drinking or smoking to cope with stress, if you are irreparably compromising your relationships and your health. Be successful, but also be clever. Make conscious money choices.

SMILE and feel AMAZING as you say:

- 'I am investing AMAZINGLY.'

- 'I have AMAZING savings.'

- 'I have plenty of money in the bank.'

- 'I have AMAZING investments.'

An investment can involve investing in a suit for an interview, a winter coat in the end-of-season sale, which will save you money the following winter (as long as you really need a new coat and can afford it at the time), a computer to run your business, a university education, going to the dentist to look after your teeth, which could cost more later if you don't take care of them, investing time building a balanced financial portfolio by seeking professional advice, buying a property in a good area, or coming up with an idea to earn money while you sleep.

Lucy, a freelance journalist who wrote an article about my client sessions and hypnotherapy recordings for increasing her wealth, decided almost immediately after her first hypnotherapy session with me to invest in a really good haircut to make her feel and look more professional. With her new haircut, she had more confidence and was able to get better-paid commissions. She also invested in more childcare for her children so that she could spend more time working, which proved to be a good investment and within the first month she was £1,000 better off.

Think about everything you spend your money on and whether it will be a good investment.

- Confront your investments and savings head on.
- Be smart – listen to other people who are successful with money.
- Do work that you believe in.
- Live in the cheapest, nicest place you can easily afford.
- Learn new skills that could lead to something worthwhile.
- Be determined and set specific goals.
- Plan and make good things happen for you.

Feel good about what you have. SMILE and feel contented about the good things in your life. Find creative ways to have just as nice a life but within your budget – maybe go out for a coffee instead of a meal, get a better deal on a holiday or go on a shorter holiday, use things you already have. And make sure that your budget takes into account money that you will put into a savings account every week or every month before you spend anything else.

Keep your mortgage manageable and have a plan to pay off the loan so that you eventually own your property. If you rent, imagine that you can find a way to pay your rent easily today and every day. If you want to buy a property, imagine that you have found AMAZING ways to buy and own your own place. Everything is possible. Your home is your foundation, so make your home affordable.

People often think that moving is expensive, but if you believe it will be AMAZING and financially fantastic for you, then it will be. A few years ago, my husband and I needed more space at home for his business and I began to look at various options that would enable us to move. I focused on it being an AMAZING move that was financially fantastic for us. Friends and family tried to convince me that moving would be expensive, but I knew that it would work out as long as I believed that an AMAZING move could happen.

After some time, I came to the conclusion that moving 10 minutes further away from London would open up a lot more properties to us that would give us the space we needed. Eventually, after doing my research and being open to an AMAZING property, we found a potentially AMAZING property that I wouldn't have looked at before. It needed some renovations, but we felt that it was worth doing the work because it was double the size of our previous home and in a gorgeous location overlooking a golf course with its own private forest. The property cost nearly £80,000 less than our other place. After moving fees and some carefully planned renovations, we had £40,000 left in the bank.

When people come to visit us in our new home they always say, 'It's AMAZING,' because it truly is a special place. And I laugh to myself, because that is what I knew it would be before we began our property search.

Doing an AMAZING property search doesn't mean an affordable dream home will just land in your lap. But if you put the work in by getting out there and viewing properties while keeping the AMAZING feeling alive and believing that there is always a way to get something AMAZING, it will lead you to that destination.

Because your home is so important, make sure that it is affordable so that you can relax in it. When you aspire to a wealthier lifestyle, rather than being desperate to have the life you haven't got yet, say, 'Maybe I could do something like that. Maybe I could have something like that.' A desperate feeling will create a desperate result. By using 'maybe', you take the urgency out of having things.

- 'Maybe I could have a car like that.'

- 'Maybe I could own a house like that.'

- 'Maybe I could be successful like her/him.'

- 'Maybe I could be a millionaire.'

- 'Maybe I could win the lottery.'

Plan the things you want to achieve financially and say, 'The money is there.' By being in the SMILE AMAZING zone, you will also find that you are in the right place at the right time for a free handout, which is a great way to boost your income. There is always someone who wants to get rid of something and somebody else who wants it. (You may find a free recycle group in your local area.)

Recently, I thought about buying a wooden swinging chair for the garden. When I went to the garden centre, I couldn't decide exactly what I wanted. So I just thought, 'Oh, it will be AMAZING. It will all sort out.'

The next day, a friend phoned to invite my husband and me for Sunday lunch a couple of weeks later. While we were there, we went into her garden, where she had a wooden swinging chair. 'I love your swinging chair,' I told our friend. 'I am going to get one soon.' 'Well, do you want mine?' she asked. 'I want to get rid of it.'

A couple of days later, my husband hired a van, picked up the garden chair and the next weekend I was swinging on it in my own garden. Our friend was happy to have got rid of it so easily, and we were delighted to be its new owners. Now, that is AMAZING!

Write clear lists of what you want in life

Set goals/dreams of what you want to achieve, from simple things like finding some garden furniture to more substantial ones, such as becoming a property owner. Write a concise list of your ideas about the life you want. Place this list somewhere your subconscious mind will see it daily, such as inside the bathroom cabinet, on the fridge, on your desk or on the wardrobe door. It is important to write the words backwards so that you can't consciously read it but your subconscious mind can. Either handwrite it or type it on the computer and then print it off. Use the word AMAZING or AMAZINGLY to make the sentences positively powerful. Soon, you will really begin to believe that you will have the items, lifestyle, job or money on your list.

Write the phrase forwards and then copy it backwards.

- AMAZING gorgeous home – emoh suoegrog GNIZAMA

- AMAZING lifestyle – elytsefil GNIZAMA

- AMAZING financial security – ytiruces laicnanif GNIZAMA

- AMAZING financial success – sseccus laicnanif GNIZAMA

- AMAZING income – emocni GNIZAMA

- AMAZING investments – stnemtsevni GNIZAMA

- AMAZING happy life – efil yppah GNIZAMA

- AMAZING dream job – boj maerd GNIZAMA

- AMAZING holiday – yadiloh GNIZAMA

- AMAZING pension provision – noisivorp noisnep GNIZAMA

Action tasks that you can do for each item on the list. For example, do research into different types of investment, see what other job opportunities are out there or look at properties as if you were ready to buy one in the area where you would like to live. Between the ages of 21 and

23, I viewed about 40 properties while looking for the most perfect cottage my husband and I could afford. When I was 23, we bought a three-bedroom cottage, which we would never have got if I had allowed myself to be put off by the fact I wasn't really ready to afford one at the beginning of the property search. But my determination was stronger than all the factors that made it seem impossible. By the time we bought the cottage we were in a good financial position to afford it and we bought the property at a reduced price as it needed renovations. If you have a dream keep investigating until you are able to make it happen.

When we think about things that are out of our reach, we put negatives in the way. When we focus on something, it begins to happen. But when we action something by pretending we are ready to make the necessary changes, it starts to feel normal and comfortable, and before you know it, it's happening. The worst thing you can do is nothing. Your investigations may make you realize that you don't actually want what you thought you wanted. If that does happen, at least you are one step closer to knowing what you *do* want.

Keep your life moving instead of feeling stuck. Imagine the path that will lead you to the wealth or the life you desire is like a wiggly string. Make your list as AMAZING as possible.

AMAZING inheritance

Be generous with your inheritance. Give money to your children and your grandchildren to help them have a better life. If you don't have children, give money to the people in your life who have made a difference to you – perhaps you have been made to feel part of someone else's family. You can stipulate how they use the money, such as for a property, holidays or education. Don't assume that people aren't struggling because they seem to be fine. Let your legacy help the next generation build something AMAZING.

SMILE about your wealth and feel AMAZING.

Chapter summary

✂ Focus on improving your wealth.

✂ Appreciate a treat when you experience it.

✂ Self-talk yourself into the positive: 'I can do it. I am doing it. It is done.'

✂ Combine the AMAZING zone with a business head.

✂ Retrain, improve your skills or follow through with an idea to increase your wealth.

✂ Write your money goals as positive statements using the word AMAZING. Write the statements backwards as well as forwards, then place the list somewhere you will see it daily.

✂ 'Snapshot' in your mind positive wealth experiences to build your AMAZING zone bank.

STEP 1. Save/invest safely and wisely.

STEP 2. Improve your income.

STEP 3. Build upon your AMAZING wealth.

Every relationship needs to be nurtured.
You can either grow apart or grow together.

CHAPTER 9

RELATIONSHIPS

The world needs different types of people for different roles, so different characteristics are important. During a recent conversation I had with a relative who is a rocket scientist, he suggested that all children should be streamed at school into engineering as there is a shortage of engineers.

'It wouldn't be the right path for everyone,' I said. 'Believe me, I wouldn't be a good engineer. It just doesn't resonate with me.' But he disagreed, saying that everyone is capable.

A few hours later, we went out shopping with several other family members, because the rocket scientist needed some new clothes. Within minutes of going into Marks and Spencer, I had arranged for a shop assistant to measure him and then picked off the shelves trousers, shirts and jackets that fitted him perfectly. My relative lives abroad, in a country where there is far less choice available in clothes shops than there is in the UK, and he was very relieved that I knew what clothes would suit him and was able to find them in the correct size. The experience rather proved my point: my relative and I have different skills, as we all do. And that's a good thing. As we agreed at the time, you certainly wouldn't want to fly to the moon in a rocket I'd designed, and you might not want my relative to choose your clothes!

But although we all have different skills, all relationships are basically the same. What I mean is, there will be some things you like about a person and there may be some things you don't like about them, or they may just see things differently from you. That's totally normal. You can't agree on everything all of the time with anyone. With some people, you will agree about more things than you disagree about; with others, you may have very few points of agreement. No one is ever going to please you all of the time, because everyone has different ways of viewing things and of reacting to life. But you can still get on with people very well if you see the differences as interesting and learn from each other.

Try not to see things as 'black and white', 'their way', 'my way' or 'one way'. Instead, remember the grey area, where solutions are found. Learn to navigate your way through all your relationships at home, at work, with family and friends by softening your views, accepting the views of other people and realizing that there are many ways to work through things. And always be open to seeing things from someone else's point of view.

The following is an example of what I mean.

Black: 'I want to book the holiday.'

White: 'I don't, so we are not going to book it.'

Grey: 'I want you to have a holiday, but I don't think we can afford *this* holiday. I am open to finding a cheaper one. To be honest, if we book a holiday that I don't feel we can comfortably pay for, I won't be able to relax and enjoy it, which would defeat the purpose of having a break.'

To diffuse an argument or disagreement you can say: 'I am different from you. You are different from me. That is why we see this issue differently. But that's okay. Let's discuss how we can work through our different opinions to find a solution we are both happy with.'

Some people are more emotional, while other people are more logical and matter of fact. Different types of traits are useful. So learn from each other to create balanced relationships. Don't see what people can't do. See what they *can* do, as these are their strengths. If different people use their different strengths, it's possible to achieve more, more easily.

Black-and-white thinking leaves no area for discussion. The grey area is the zone where you will sort through things. A healthy relationship is one in which both parties are open to discussion.

Say to yourself, 'I can make this relationship work. It is working.' Or, 'I can find AMAZING ways to communicate well with my partner.' You will probably find ways to sort things out, even if you and your partner don't agree.

Too many people spend too much time complaining and focusing on what doesn't work rather than on what *is* working within a relationship or on finding solutions to work through things.

Photo album technique

See past events as old photographs in your mind being filed into the appropriate albums so that you can archive them and move on. You can choose to forgive for whatever has happened in your past. You don't need approval from anyone but yourself. Then see your past and future as a solid path of stepping stones. When you let go of the negative, you will be able to create an AMAZING relationship. You and your partner have probably achieved quite a lot together. Start to feel good about the good things and make a list of the things that don't work so well. Then work through each item that needs improvement. Sit down together to discuss how you can both improve the situation.

So much of the niggling bad feeling that exists between people is caused by ridiculous things, such as how much milk someone puts in their tea, or sugar in their coffee or salt on their food. Everyone has different tastes in food and drinks, as they do in life in general, too. Try to respect this and to enjoy the things you have in common with those around you. Most issues are resolvable, so choose to work through problems. Only when you have tried everything should you go your separate ways. If you try to run away from your problems, they will simply follow you.

A typical example is a husband who can't face family life and arguments with his wife. He decides to run off with a younger woman, who later wants to have children – and he ends up in the same situation with another young family.

- Anger = hostility = distress
- Discussion = solutions = happiness

Relaxation technique

Try to relax by breathing calmly, allowing tensions to dissolve by imagining your problems drifting like clouds in the sky. Take a few deep breaths in and out and, once the storm clouds have dispersed, you can begin to have reasonable discussions again.

You and your partner have created behaviour patterns that will repeat themselves if you let them. Instead of being frustrated by the repetition of old behaviour, work out why it is happening and find a way to do things differently. Allow your mind to come up with solutions. Remember, there is always a better way. Say 'It's all fine. It's all resolving.'

Most of the old issues that people in long-term relationships focus on don't even exist any more. Imagine these issues dissolving like clouds evaporating. We become programmed to repeat behaviour we have learned, so similar problems may have cropped up again and again. Allow new positive habits and patterns to form between you and your partner.

Let go of events in the past that perhaps your partner can't let go of. Rub, press or tap the knuckles on your left hand using the fingers of your right hand. The past might have been stressful, but it is only the events of today that you need to deal with. Take each day moment by moment. Don't engage in battles. Doing so will only fuel a negative, destructive fire. Instead, diffuse situations as if you were dampening a fire with cool, calming water. You can close your eyes when you repeat this technique.

- Lower expectations of each other.

- Work together as a team.

- Encourage each other.

- Praise each other.

- Presume things will work out AMAZINGLY well.

- Be yourself but be flexible within your relationship.

Life is a series of beginnings and endings. So embrace where you are with each person in your life, knowing that any bad feelings within the relationship can end and comfortable feelings can begin at any point. Do your best to get your relationships into a positive place for you. Use the AMAZING to feel things working out well. Feel free and let others be free too. Help other people to see the way through things as you learn yourself.

I have helped many clients over the years to see their relationships differently, and most people have gone on to have very happy relationships once they have let go of the tensions that had built up.

Anyone is capable of being stuck in their own ways. Ask yourself, 'What can I change about myself? How can I improve who I am? What can I do to improve my relationships?' As you change for the better, those around you will change too as you create new habits of communication between you. You can't change others, but you can change yourself.

Watching technique

Try to be in the moment. Instead of being bored or stressed by the person you are listening to, watch their lips moving.

You will find you enjoy watching their enjoyment, as they tell you what they have to say. SMILE to yourself. Enjoy seeing other people happy to be speaking. Let other people's conversations relax you. Be interested in other people, even if they are talking about something that isn't of any interest to you, for example football, shoes, dance, computer games...

From time to time, try something your partner likes and you might find that you actually quite enjoy it too. For example, you might not like scented candles, but you may find you don't mind them when you are feeling more relaxed. Or you might not like watching sport, but if you and your partner sit together occasionally, you might find you enjoy it. If you like different things, then both find the time to pursue your own interests as well as doing things together. If one of you wants to go shopping and the other wants to watch sport, each of you do your own thing and then meet up for a coffee afterwards. But if your help is needed, be there for your partner. It is all about balance. No one can do everything they want all of the time.

Think about the different strengths you and your partner bring to your relationship. Perhaps one of you is more technical, creative, practical or organized. In a work environment, companies employ people who are good at whatever their particular job requires them to do. In a relationship, decide which of you is good at which jobs and then divide up the tasks so that each of you is doing the ones you are good at or don't mind doing. The tasks that neither of you has any interest in or ability for will have to be shared. Do those tasks together or pay someone else to do them.

If you both stick to these principles, you can overcome a lot of the irritation caused by everyday tasks. The difficulties arise when one person in the relationship is unable to be flexible or is unwilling to see both sides of a situation. When that happens, you may end up in stalemate. If you are struggling to communicate with your partner, try all the techniques in this book. Most people can resolve their relationships. If yours can be fixed, it will be. If not, you will both have to move on.

Don't be tricked into thinking that the grass is greener on the other side of the fence. You could find yourself in a similar situation. Perhaps you were half the problem. Sort out your problems and help your partner to sort out theirs by working together. Be spontaneous. Get out of any ruts you may be in. Be happy in yourself.

Meetings

Support your partner in every way – in work, at home and with your children. Have a meeting to discuss what needs to be said, just as you would have an appraisal at work. That way, you can bring things up in a controlled setting. Whatever goes on in the meeting can remain in the meeting, rather than allowing the emotions to be carried with you into your everyday life.

In any relationship, there will be difficult issues that may need to be addressed, so accept this and deal with them in a calm way. Then put closure on the discussion. Try to leave any bad feelings in the meeting. It isn't always possible, but it will become easier as you get used to dealing with life this way.

You can also say to yourself, 'Cut the crap and feel AMAZING,' knowing things will work out AMAZINGLY well as the result of making lots of small changes.

Sex life

Both men and women can feel dissatisfied with the sex within their marriage or partnership. Don't think that an affair will solve your problems. It won't. If you build your relationship from the roots up, you will build an interesting, strong relationship. Look at the good things about you and your partner and work through the things that you both need to change. It may be a series of choices and decisions that have blown your relationship off course. So it is through new choices and decisions that you can get it back on course again and keep it there. If you do things differently, you will get out of the rut and create a relationship with a sparkle. 'Snapshot' in your mind the good times you create from now onwards so that you build a bank of AMAZING zone relationship feelings.

At the end of the day, all relationships are about feeling comfy with your slippers on and eating dinner together. British comedian Russell Brand once said in an interview when asked about what it was like to live with American singer Katy Perry, 'It is just the same as anyone else, talking about everyday things such as "Do you think the cat needs to go to the vet?"'

If you are not sexually compatible, find ways to change that, such as massage or dancing to your favourite love songs with no sexual pressure. Tell your partner regularly how beautiful/handsome they are. Talk about the fun you had when you first met and make new, happy memories by going to nice places together. Remind each other of the things you like about each other. Build trust.

Learn to be close without expecting to have sex and eventually, in most cases, if you don't put pressure on your partner, it will develop. Tell your partner, 'I don't want sex. I just want a cuddle.' After cuddling, leave them wanting more. People are not machines that can be turned on and off.

Many arguments arise because people are distracted by the things going on around them, by technology, sport, kids, work, family or friends. When that happens, it may be that the only time someone pays any attention to their partner is when they want sex, which is very off-putting. Or maybe they don't want sex with their partner because they are tired or cross with them. Agree to stop insulting each other or saying things that are insulting to men or women.

Invest time in developing your relationship with your partner so that you reap the rewards of intimate sexual experiences. A relationship is like a flower bud that opens when the sun is shining but may not do so if the sun is blocked by a cloud. A flower also needs bees to pollinate it and rainwater to help it grow and develop. If all these elements are not right, the flower will not fully open. You and your partner also need all the elements to be right, but for you the elements include kindness, romance, listening to each other, supporting each other and helping each other.

Don't expect your partner to think and feel like you do. Discuss what you both like, if it feels comfortable to do so. Too many relationships are affected by pornography, which is not what gives couples long-term satisfying, intimate experiences. Instead, try to find educational information on the internet that will enable you to develop your knowledge of how your partner's body works. Experiment with new ways of turning your partner on and making love to them. Pornography presents a distorted reality of what a healthy sex life is. So let go of everything you may have learned from it. You may have fun with it from time to time, but to build a strong foundation for a sexual relationship:

- Think romantic comedy not pornography.

- Try making love to romantic music, which will help you to create new habits and patterns related to your sex life.

- Doing things differently will create different results.

- By making new choices and decisions together, you can build an AMAZING relationship.

Romantic gestures

Discuss with each other what type of romantic gestures you both like. Some people like being bought a thoughtful gift, while others may prefer a verbal compliment, having a meal made for them or a hug. Basically, listen to your partner and be aware when they are doing something nice for you that you previously may have taken for granted.

You can research online for ideas about romantic things you could do. By investing a little bit of time in arranging romance, you will reap the reward of a happier relationship.

- Buy your partner a food treat they love.

- Message your partner telling them you love them or that you are looking forward to seeing them.

- Book a surprise meal or weekend break somewhere your partner would like to go.

- Teach each other to cook something.

- Give your partner a massage.

- Play your partner's favourite music.

- Arrange for a practical chore to be done, such as fixing the laptop or decorating a room.

If your partner asks what you would like for your birthday, don't say 'Nothing' when you are secretly hoping for a surprise. Guide your partner to buy things from a shop you like so that they will buy something you want. You could both write lists of the type of things you would like to receive as gifts, such as technology gadgets, perfume, aftershave or concert tickets.

If your partner arranges a romantic gesture for you, be pleased with whatever it is. Even if it isn't something you would have chosen for yourself, be appreciative and don't throw the gesture back in their face. If you listen to each other, you'll each find out what the other person likes. But if your partner forgets an event such as an anniversary, forgive them and arrange to celebrate it on another day.

Planning ahead is easy when you can order gifts and cards online. Don't wait for your partner to be romantic. Romantic surprises should be fun and they don't need to cost much. A heart-shaped piece of toast, a love note in an underwear drawer, on a pillow or in a packed lunch, a cake or some rose petals scattered around a candlelit bath are all inexpensive ways to be romantic. But everyone is different, so get to know what types of things your partner likes. There is no point sending them skydiving as a treat if it is really something you want to do and they would hate it!

If you listen to what your partner has to say, you will gradually become harmonious together. Teach your children to be romantic with their partner when they grow up by setting a good example now. If you explain to your children how important it is to put effort into their relationships later, it will feel natural to them rather than being a chore.

Sharing responsibility for your children

Be reasonable with your partner. You should both be able to take breaks from caring for your children if you help each other out. If you are both working, do as much as you can to support each other. If you are a stay-at-home mum or dad, give your partner some breathing space when they return home from work. Give them time to take a shower or make a cup of tea before you bombard them with a running commentary of your day's events or before you expect them to help you do whatever needs to be done in the house. Clients often complain that their spouses expect them to take over the care of the children the moment they walk in the door. Try to be more organized so that you can all have quality time together as a family. If you are divorced, still do your share to give your partner a proper break and thank them for the money they give for the children or for the work they do in looking after them.

Let go of the fear

Eliminate your problems and then see what you are left with. Don't let simple decisions like 'Should we let the kids get a hamster?' become a battleground. Live in the moment. Don't make a drama out of small issues. Try to look at the bigger scheme of things. Trust that you both have good ideas and sometimes flow with your partner's ideas to see where they lead.

Some time ago, my husband and I lived in Shanghai for a year, during which time I came across a little dog that needed a home. I was being practical, thinking through how we would get the dog back to the UK without having to put him in quarantine. But my husband said, 'Just get him. We'll find a way. And if we can't keep him, we will find him a better home. Either way, he'll be better off than he is now.' So we got the dog and everything worked out fine, because we found a family in France who looked after him for six months so he could gain entry to the UK without going into quarantine. It was a great decision to get the dog. It all worked out AMAZINGLY well – for the dog and for us!

Respect each other's individuality. Be inspired by your partner and teach them to be inspired by you too. It doesn't really matter what you do in life as long as you are happy. If your partner wants something that will make them happy (within budget), you may also end up benefiting from it. So be agreeable to giving the idea a go.

Try to say to your partner, 'Do what you think. I am sure you will make good decisions.' And think to yourself, 'It will work out AMAZINGLY well.' Once the tension between you dissolves, your partner may decide not to go ahead with whatever they were thinking about doing. If so, they will have come to that conclusion on their own and won't blame you later for any consequences. It will also avoid negative wasted energy, which can be very draining on a relationship.

If your partner won't let you do something, let go of needing it and say to yourself, 'Maybe it will happen. It will work out AMAZINGLY well.' Once you let go, you may find that you don't want to do it as much as you thought you did, or your partner may become more open to you going ahead with whatever it is.

- Flexibility and an open mind on both sides will create a flowing relationship.

- Take responsibility for yourself by tidying up after yourself in the kitchen and bathroom, making the bed and picking up your clothes.

- Be responsible with money by staying within budget.

- Do your share of household tasks.

- Be romantic.

Make a list of things you can improve on in your relationships. Look at the list and see which items you can sort out. Keep ticking things off the list and add to it so that you deal with issues as they arise instead of letting them build up. Different things will be relevant at different stages of your life. Dip in and out of the list and find creative ways to sort things out AMAZINGLY.

- Create positive self-talk in your mind about your relationship.

Praise goes a long way

Everyone loves being praised and feeling special. Notice the things people can do and point out to them how well they are doing them. Be interested in other people, ask them questions about themselves and be interested in what they have to say. Add to conversations by mentioning relevant things that help to keep the conversation flowing. No one wants to be around people who talk about themselves without being interested in other people too. Have two-way conversations – think of it as traffic on a motorway with vehicles going in both directions.

Separation/divorce

Try to sort out your relationship using the rules in this and the following chapter and throughout this book. Remember, running from a relationship may not be the answer. You could end up with similar problems in another relationship or there may be so much fallout from the split that you hardly gain. You may think that getting divorced will resolve your problems. But, if you have children together, any friction that exists between you and your ex-partner could make your children feel like 'piggy in the middle'. Or your ex-partner may go on to have a new relationship and your children may not like the new step-parent. So try to resolve your marriage before you split – unless, of course, you are in danger. Do everything you can to get back on track, as most relationships are resolvable if you can both be reasonable and see each other's point of view.

- Leaving is not always the solution. But staying together isn't always the solution either.

- Presume things will work out AMAZINGLY well and flow with what is best for you at each stage.

Improving your relationship

In a marriage or with a live-in partner, try to live like students or young friends sharing accommodation: be free individuals who don't try to own or control each other. Do your share of what needs to be done, just as students have to pull their weight because if they don't, no one will want to live with them for the next year.

Say to your partner, even if only jokingly, 'You are an AMAZING man/woman, so kind, so loving.' When they hear this positive message and you hear yourself saying the words, you will both begin to change. Learn to laugh and give your partner the opportunity to get it right next time.

Support your partner to fulfil their dreams and ask them to allow you to achieve your dreams too. Allow your ideas to flourish. If your partner wants to have an art studio at home, help them create the space to do their art. If your partner wants to go on a hiking holiday, help them to choose the perfect rucksack. Find a way to really live your lives and don't hinder each other's goals. When you both feel free in a relationship, you will both be happy.

My partner loves me

You could buy each other a special mug. Choose the mugs separately and try to get one that you imagine your partner would love. Imagine they think it is AMAZING. Accept whatever mug your partner buys for you and call it your 'My husband loves me mug' or 'My wife loves me mug' or 'My partner loves me mug'. Every time you drink your coffee or tea out of it, say to yourself, 'My husband loves me' or 'My wife loves me' or 'My partner loves me'.

Be relaxed about presents. Get some clues about what your partner likes and buy something you think they would love. Keep the presents small. If there's something either of you wants or needs, buy it for yourself instead of expecting someone else to read your mind. This way you will be happy.

Don't let others disappoint you. If you want an AMAZING birthday, organize it yourself: only you know what you really want. Don't just say 'AMAZING birthday'. Pick up the phone, invite your friends and book a restaurant, book paint-balling, a spa day or a golf tournament. Take control of your own happiness.

Chocolate brownie technique

Try to speak positively. No one responds well to criticism. Start with something positive and end on a positive too: 'You are doing really well with ... I need to tell you ... You could try to do this ... Anyway, keep up the good work.' You can say the same thing either positively or negatively. A chocolate brownie can be light, soft and gooey straight from the oven, but if it comes out of a fridge, it can be cold, solid and heavy: you are eating the same thing but having two completely different experiences. Think about the chocolate brownie when you speak to people. Are you bringing out in them the warm, soft gooeyness or the cold, solid heaviness?

- Speak in a nice way to create AMAZING relationships.

Let go of the past

Let go of past relationships. If they had been meant to be, they would have been. Too many people hold on to old relationships that clutter up their mind and stop them moving on, which can affect new relationships. Life is all about constantly moving on – from nursery to junior school to senior school and then to the workplace. And every time we move on, people come in and out of our lives. See today as an adventure and as an opportunity for new and better relationships to come your way. Life is a journey that keeps getting better and better if we allow it to.

Beware of bullies

Bullies at school may go on to be bullies at work, at home and in relationships. Be aware of whether you are bullying or whether someone in your life is bullying you. The best way to deal with a bully is to accept that this is who they are so that you can try to understand the way they think. They are probably living in the black-and-white zone without seeing the grey area of different options, e.g. 'You should be doing or seeing things my way.' In your mind, turn their comments into humour and see the situation as a cartoon.

Learn to stand up for yourself by working on your own self-belief and by improving the way you approach conversations, so that you explain things in a way other people can understand. For example, 'We see this point differently because we are different people.' Empower yourself by feeling good about yourself and believing in yourself.

If someone asks a question, it is because they don't know the answer. A bully may sneer at the question, implying that the person should know the answer. Bullies have got themselves into bad habits of behaving badly. So be aware of their problems by noticing their behaviour and the way they speak to you and to other people.

Presume that things will work out AMAZINGLY well as you think them through with a SMILE. Break the habit of being bullied by laughing to yourself, as if the bully is in a TV sitcom. Allow any bad experience to empower you to propel yourself forwards to another level of positive.

- Some people will deliberately bully.

- Some people are unaware that their behaviour is affecting other people.

- Some people are so aware of other people that they are unable to do anything because they don't want to offend anyone, which can make them more susceptible to being bullied.

Do things differently

If you have difficult friends/family members who drain you or who you find to be negative, try to think of new ways to meet up. For example, go out for the day so that your conversations are about the day out and not about their problems. Go to the theatre or a museum or on a boat trip or do anything else that inspires you. If you really can't bear to be in their company, set them free and set yourself free by honouring your feelings and being around the people who suit you best. If someone is good for you, they will come back into your life at an appropriate time.

Relationships with good friends

Friends will come in and out of your life and your partner's life. Good friends will always 'feel' right when you see them. Don't force friendships or feel let down if a friend is in a different headspace at a particular time. Set your friends free and, like boomerangs, they will come back into your life when the time is right.

As you become more positive, some of your friends may not feel comfortable being around your positivity, and you may not feel comfortable with their negativity. But they may become more positive in the future, so always leave the door open for them to come back into your life.

Speak-to-a-photo technique

Try talking to a photograph of the person you want to speak to, perhaps your husband/wife, friend, work colleague or child. It is a good idea to get things off your chest before you actually speak to them in person. Once you have told the photograph everything you want to say, you may find that there is no need to have a discussion with the person themselves. When you do see them, you will be calmer and more rational and you may feel that the air has already cleared.

Make special time for yourself and for each person in your life and feel AMAZING.

Chapter summary

✂ Use the relaxation technique: let the problems pass. Say, 'It's all fine. It's all resolving.'

✂ Use the watching technique: enjoy watching people tell you about the things they are interested in.

✂ Have a meeting to discuss issues calmly.

✂ Be romantic with your partner.

✂ Get to know what your partner likes.

✂ Praise people – everyone likes to feels special.

✂ Use the chocolate brownie technique: bring out the warmth in people, not the cold.

STEP 1. Let go of rigid black-and-white thinking.

STEP 2. Remember everyone is individual.

STEP 3. Focus on people's strengths.

*Choices and decisions create
a good or bad relationship.*

CHAPTER 10

RELATIONSHIP
RULES

All good relationships are about sticking to a set of rules

- It is us, not other people, who are in control of our relationships, of whether or not we are prepared to put up with something, or have the ability to work through issues, or expect too much or too little. Try to be balanced and always imagine finding a way through things so that they work out well. But be prepared for the fact that some things can't be fixed.

- Remember the grey area where the solutions are found. Avoid black-and-white thinking.

- Love yourself enough not to let the behaviour of others affect you. It doesn't matter what people say or do, you can still feel good about yourself. Say to yourself, 'I am AMAZING' and 'They are AMAZING,' as this will dissolve the negative between you.

- Other people are AMAZING too. SMILE and imagine that you bring out the AMAZING in them.

- Be open to other people's ideas and opinions and remember that there are many ways to do things, not just one way. Work *with* others, not against them. Remind them that you may see some things differently from the way they see them.

- Don't spend time worrying about other people's problems. Imagine things have worked out AMAZINGLY well for them and let them get on with sorting out their own lives.

- Don't rescue other people. Instead, rescue yourself. Every time you sort something out for someone else, they don't have to learn how to do it themselves. Rescuing them only delays their development.

- Say to yourself and to other people, 'You can and you will sort this out. You are good at sorting things out.' It is okay to help people if they are helping themselves too.

- Don't buy into negative dramas. Instead, be around positive people.

- Some people are logical in their thinking, some are emotional and some are creative. We need all types of people to make the world go round. If we all thought the same way, it would be impossible to function as a society. Be interested by your partner and by the people around you and appreciate their special qualities.

- SMILE at the past. See it as a sitcom and laugh at it. Laughter brings you into a positive 'now'.

- If someone is being difficult, instead of getting angry, just SMILE to yourself and imagine you are in a comedy film.

- If you are the 'difficult one' in a relationship, sort out your problems. For instance, do you drink a lot? Are you untidy? Are you demanding? Do you talk about things that you never do? Do you live your life through other people's achievements? Do you gossip negatively? Do you believe that you are better than everyone else? Are you annoying? Are you lazy? Are you hyperactive? Look at yourself and become a better version of you. Take on board other people's comments and suggestions. Listen, be open and decide whether there is something about your behaviour that you need to change so that you and those around you will reap the benefits.

- Once you have made any necessary improvements to your behaviour, be yourself and allow other people to be themselves.

- Listen to what other people have to say, but encourage them to make the right choices for themselves. And make the right choices for yourself, too.

- Don't share your ideas with other people who may convince you not to do something you were planning to do. Trust your own gut feelings. Many people miss opportunities and never do what feels right because they are put off by other people before they even get started.

- You create your own destiny by believing in yourself and making things happen. You can change your direction in a split second by believing that AMAZIING things will happen and by actioning what needs to be done. Be firm in your own mind about what you want, then go out and make it happen. Listen to yourself, and if you hear your negative voice, change it to positive talk so that better things can happen.

- Get the right balance between voicing your opinions and keeping them to yourself. If you don't like other people's opinions, understand that it is just their viewpoint. You don't have to agree with them, but you don't need to tell them when you disagree, and risk insulting them unnecessarily.

- Treat people with respect. Always speak on the same level.

- If someone is aggressive or threatening, seek professional advice about how best to cope with the situation.

- Accept kindness from other people and be kind to them. Be respectful of yourself, other people, animals and the environment you are in.

- You wouldn't tell your neighbour how to cut their grass. Treat family members the same way. Don't tell people what to do or how to live their lives. Let your children, family and spouse be themselves in your company. Explain the rules and why they are necessary, but speak to your family members like you would speak to a neighbour. You don't own anyone.

- Everyone has strengths. See the strengths in people close to you. Don't expect them to be good at everything you are good at. Remember, we are all individuals. Work together and bring your individual strengths to your relationships.

- If you are not happy about something your spouse or child has or hasn't done, have a meeting to discuss things calmly and feel the relaxed feeling of AMAZING solutions working out well. Try to enjoy every phase of your life by sorting things out as they arise.

- Think of 10 things you like about each person in your life, at home and at work. This will help you to see the positive in everyone.

- When things are going well with people, 'snapshot' the moment in your mind to add to your AMAZING zone memory bank.

- Accept that everyone is on their own path, which may be different from yours. Allow other people to make their own decisions, just as you make yours.

- A joke is only funny if the person on the receiving end of it finds it funny.

- You may need to tell a small white lie to avoid offending someone. But if you are telling lies regularly, you need to ask yourself why you need to lie and what it is about your life that you need to change.

- In any relationship, you are both right and you are both wrong. You both see things your own way.

- If you are in a challenging relationship, either personally or professionally, feel the feeling of it working out AMAZINGLY well. This may mean that you go in separate directions or that you resolve whatever the problem is. Say to yourself, 'Maybe this will work out AMAZINGLY well.'

STEP 1. Allow your AMAZINGness to flourish.

STEP 2. Allow the AMAZINGness of other people to flourish.

STEP 3. Imagine things working out AMAZINGLY.

*Cut the stress and create an AMAZINGLY
calm life for yourself and those around you.*

CHAPTER 11

STRESS, REST AND
RELAXATION

You create your crazy life

The pace of life in recent years has become even faster. We live in a go, go, go society where more demands are put on people to work longer hours and get more done in less time, where we – and other people – have high expectations of ourselves and where technology fills up any spare time we might otherwise have had. One of the most important things you can do for yourself is simplify your life to eliminate your stresses.

- De-stress your diary. Be selective about who you see and what you do.

- Plan ahead and be organized.

- Put technology down and ban it from the bedroom.

- Make a conscious effort to be in the moment rather than worrying about things in the future.

- Stop rushing when it is not necessary. Try to pull back within yourself to stay calm.

- Turn your go, go, go life into a slow, slow, slow life, making time to relax.

- Say 'No' to things that will push up your stress levels or put you under pressure.

- Switch off from work and ignore work communications in your spare time.

- Reclaim your quiet time. Reclaim your sanity.

- Minimize the amount of news you watch, as this can be negative and stressful.

- Get in control of your debt and finances.

Most stress is a build-up of many small things that can easily be sorted out. Identify the things you can change in your week to ease any pressure. What are the difficult times during your week? What are the things that stress you most? Identify the stresses and then try to find solutions to these problems. There are always solutions. There is always another way of doing something.

If you have too much stress in your life, it may cause you to sink into depressed or anxious feelings, making you more tired and exhausted. Don't make excuses about why you have to put up with the way things are. You might not find solutions immediately, but, by identifying the problems, you will begin to find answers that will help you to make the right changes.

The following list will help you identify the stresses in your life.

- Too much work tension?

- Financially stretched?

- Just about coping with life?

- Too busy?

- Too lonely?

- Addictions: alcohol, smoking, drugs?

- Feel trapped in your life?

- Relationship issues?

- Struggling with parenting?

- Health issues?

- Exam worries?

- Career stress?

- Family problems?

Write down your problems and then write down the answers to solving each issue. Learn to self-talk yourself into the positive. Most of the things you feel stressed about are very easy to resolve. If you don't know the answer today, go back to that question another time. You can write down these questions and answers regularly to stop stresses building up. By doing this, you will take the emotions out of the problem, which will allow you to come up with a rational solution. Letting go of repeated negative thoughts will relax your mind. You will feel better and be more focused, and therefore more able to move things forwards.

The following are some stress examples. Use them to help you see how you could find creative solutions that will enable you to let go of your stresses.

1. *Problem:* It doesn't matter how much I earn, I don't seem to have enough money.

    Solution: Like most people, you have probably overstretched yourself with your expenses. Not saving any money, lack of planning and thinking that it will be all right to make impulsive purchases may have caught up with you. Start to make a plan of where you can cut back and begin to save. Set up a savings account to save for birthdays, Christmases and holidays.

2. *Problem:* I get stressed about having midweek drinks with colleagues or clients because it means I get home too late, and the alcohol is not good for me on a work night.

    Solution: Start with a soft drink, have one alcoholic drink, then make an excuse and leave. By the time the other people have had a couple of alcoholic drinks, they won't even notice you are departing early. Imagine you get home completely sober at a reasonable time feeling healthy and AMAZING.

3. *Problem:* I feel stressed and drained by friends or family problems.

Solution: Pretend that you are busy so that you don't get caught up in their latest drama. You are entitled to a life yourself, so learn to let other people sort out their own problems. Tell them that they can and will sort things out themselves. Then feel good about yourself for having the confidence to let others take responsibility for their own situations.

4. *Problem:* I feel stressed and dread Wednesdays because the kids have too many activities to go to after school, which makes fitting in mealtime a nightmare.

   Solution: Share the pick-ups and drop-offs of your kids with other parents. Prepare an easy meal in advance so that it is simple to feed everyone at the appropriate times. Choose food that will be easy to heat up, such as a casserole. Imagine Wednesdays are easy and AMAZING.

5. *Problem:* I can't cope with deadlines, exam or study/work stress. They cause me so much worry.

   Solution: Rearrange your diary during the week. Think of your deadline as being a day or two before it actually is so that you use your time more efficiently. Repeat to yourself, 'I can do it. I am doing it. It is done.' Visualize your completed work and see yourself in your mind relaxed on the day before the deadline, with everything having been achieved easily on time. Imagine you are celebrating your great results/grades.

When you feel yourself tense or stressed, remember to find another way

If you have ever been to London, you may have noticed that as soon as you enter the Underground you walk at the fast pace of everyone else, even if you are not in a rush. Be aware and slow your life down. It is your choice how you live your life. So stop running around like a headless chicken and set boundaries of what is acceptable for you to cope with. Allow the world to revolve around you rather than you revolving around the world. It will still continue to turn on its axis whether you are stressed or not.

Perfectionism is useful for certain things, for instance if you want to be a top athlete and in some work settings. But in most other situations it can become a burden that can wear you out and drive those around you mad. Stop micro-managing your life and everyone else's. Learn to let things go. If you want to live a relaxed life, start making it relaxed by adjusting your attitude.

Learn to relax

Start living the life you want to live by taking time to rest. Listen to the way you speak to yourself and to other people. Notice when there is unnecessary urgency in your voice and then soften and slow your speech. It is all the small stresses in your day that result in you feeling and being stressed.

Learn from other people how they relax. Many years ago, I stayed with friends in France who had two young children at the time. On Saturday afternoons, the whole family went to their bedrooms for a quiet time or to sleep. I adopted the same routine when I was a busy working mum and didn't feel guilty at the weekend if I needed a rest, especially if I had a long evening ahead or if I just wanted to catch up after a busy week.

Try to flow with what your body is telling you. If you need to rest, then rest. It is very simple. Also, repeat to yourself, 'I can find AMAZING ways to relax,' and before long you will have created a good relaxation routine that suits you. And when you are more relaxed, those around you will be too. Soon you will be making AMAZING adjustments to the way you do things.

These suggestions and the tips on the next page may sound like common sense, but many people are rushing too much to remember to do them.

- Change your clothes after your working day finishes.

- Have a shower or bath after work.

- Drink camomile tea and put lavender scent in your pillow.

- Exercise at home – yoga moves, push ups, whatever you like.

- Go for a walk every day.

- Listen to your favourite music.

- Listen to calming music.

- Speak calmly.

- Move calmly.

- Fill your home and workplace with calming words such as love, rest, relaxation, calm, happy home (on your desk, on cushions, as framed pictures).

- Rest more.

- SMILE.

Let your mind offload its stresses before you go to sleep. Many people rush around all day at 100 miles per hour, then watch TV and go straight to bed, with no time just to be with themselves and let their mind unwind.

Offloading your stresses technique

Take 5-10 minutes every day to relax your mind. Talk calmly to yourself in your head about your day tomorrow so that you feel fully prepared: 'I will get it done. I will have an AMAZING day.' Feel the positive feeling of tomorrow having gone well as you SMILE. With your eyes closed, imagine things going well. You can move your eyes from left to right, up and down, and rotate them in a circular motion, feeling the calm, good feelings with your eyes in all positions. This will release tension around your eyes and help you to believe in the changes you want to make. You may find falling asleep to calming music will help you sleep deeply.

You can repeat these phrases: 'Life is easy. Life is calm. I sleep well. I am an AMAZING sleeper. I am fine. I am relaxed.'

Before you go to bed, write down anything you need to do the next day so that you are not worrying about it as you go to sleep. You can keep a pen beside your bed in case you think of something in the night. It is better to write things down rather than worry about them.

Daily de-stress technique

At intervals throughout the day, take a moment to feel calm by being aware of your breathing. Be aware of being in your body. Be aware of your surroundings. Be aware of colours. Be aware of how your clothes feel against your skin. Be aware of the feel of the seat you are sitting on or the feel of your shoes against your feet. Be aware of the sounds and smells around you. By being aware, you will be distracted from any stresses and will feel more in the moment and calmer.

In the morning, be dynamic. Start the day focused and with positive self-talk in your mind, rather than with a relaxation meditation. I suggest if you wish to meditate, do it after your work has finished so that you can relax and offload your stress. But find what works for you.

When you think you can't keep going, remind yourself that you can and, by making lots of small changes in the way you do things and the way you feel, you will find a way.

Cut the stress from your life and feel AMAZING.

Chapter summary

✂ Choose to live your life calmly.

✂ Make a list of ways in which you can improve your week.

✂ Create a daily relaxation routine.

✂ Allow your mind to offload your day before you go to sleep.

✂ Keep a pen beside your bed and write down things that you need to do tomorrow.

✂ Enjoy just being in your body.

STEP 1. Identify stress.

STEP 2. Eliminate stress.

STEP 3. Learn to relax.

Protect your health, work with the body you have and find solutions that will enable you to be as well as you can be.

CHAPTER 12

HEALTH

Your body is part of nature, a complex ecosystem within itself. In fact, we will all dissolve back into the ground eventually, one way or another. Like nature, your body is constantly evolving and responding to the environment around it and to what you put into it. If you bombard your body with harsh chemicals, excess alcohol, poor nutrition and stress, it will have to work even harder to protect and repair itself.

Most people take their body for granted until some part of it fails. That failure can be difficult to accept. Your body and the way it works – or doesn't work – are partly the product of your genetic make-up and partly due to the things you do with it and for it, such as whether you minimize stress and look after yourself as best you can.

Accept where your health is right NOW. Whether you are well or not, accept it and say to yourself, 'This is where I am right now.' From now onwards, through a series of new choices and decisions, you can do your best to improve and protect your health. To be able to live any kind of life, you need your body. So taking charge of your wellbeing is a priority.

Everyone will know someone who has been affected by a health issue at some time or another, or you may be going through health problems yourself right now. Try to feel that things will work out AMAZINGLY well. Create a sense of inner warmth, of things being fine no matter what is going on. SMILE as you focus on finding solutions. There isn't one magic answer, but there is a series of things you can do that will all contribute to getting better. I call it the percentage rule: one thing may help 10%, another 5%, another 20%, and before you know it, you will be almost 50% better. You need to put into your body and into your life everything that could help you get better and eliminate everything that may be causing your ill-health.

Remove from your life:

- Stress (which is a health hazard)
- Bad food
- Alcohol
- Cigarettes
- Late nights
- Worries/anxiety
- Poor sleep
- Toxic relationships

Add into your life:

- Looking after yourself
- Healthy nutrition and drinks
- Pamper evenings/spa days
- Exercise/sport
- Relaxing music
- Things that make you laugh
- Rest
- Good-quality sleep
- Positive visualization of you being well
- Positive language: 'I am as healthy as I can be,' and 'It is working out AMAZINGLY well.'

Health anxiety

To get over any health anxieties, use the clouds-in-the-sky technique. Rub or press your left knuckles using the fingers of your right hand and imagine the stress or worry passing like clouds in the sky. Also visualize a red triangle in your mind, put the fears into it and shrink it down.

Try to see this health journey as an adventure on which you will meet AMAZING people along the way. You will have AMAZING tests, which will help you get the correct diagnosis, and you will find out what is wrong in the best way so that you can get AMAZING treatments and solutions to help you through this phase of your life. You will enter into a whole new world and you will enjoy the experience.

People often fear medical tests, but each time you have a scan, blood test or any other diagnostic test, say to yourself, 'This is AMAZING for me. This is good for me. This is helping me get as well as I can be.' If you are receiving treatment, say, 'My body is responding AMAZINGLY well to this treatment.'

Imagine a year from now when everything has worked out AMAZINGLY well. Focus on the day after the procedure, operation or treatment as if it has all gone AMAZINGLY well. This will help create a bright future in your mind and bypass all the 'what if' worries. Say, 'What if it is AMAZING?'

If you do receive a difficult diagnosis, you can still imagine it has worked out as AMAZINGLY as it could have done, and you may be pleasantly surprised – maybe because you are offered a revolutionary new treatment. Do everything you can to improve your condition and think AMAZING as much as possible. Keeping calm will be beneficial to your health.

Wave technique

Imagine being on a beach at the water's edge. Imagine the gentle waves washing in and out. Be aware of the flow of the water and the movement of each wave. Every wave is different. Every wave is fluid. Every wave is moving. Just as each day is different and flowing, your body is different from everyone else's and you can find what is best for you. Flow with the treatment. Flow with any tests. Flow with life and solutions. There is always something to discover, so be open to opportunities that might come your way. Repeat the technique any time you think about health issues.

Try to enjoy every day as best you can. Try to find positives in your life, even with an illness to cope with.

I was helping a friend who was going through a health scare. 'Start really living every day from now onwards,' I told her. 'Get yourself a napkin holder, fill it with beautiful, colourful paper napkins and use them every day as a reminder that today is special. Don't wait for birthdays and holidays to use a nice napkin. Live in the moment.'

You may wonder how this could help but, for many people, using a nice napkin really does feel special. As the napkins sit on the table, you will see them every day, and as mealtimes occur every day too, you will be reminded regularly to be positive. The napkins will help to distract your focus from any negative things going on around you. My friend said that seeing them on the table was comforting and made her feel positive about her situation. She took a photograph of them so that she could look at it when she was out and remind herself, wherever she was, to say, 'Things will work out AMAZINGLY well.'

What are you waiting for? Feel AMAZING every time you pick up a napkin and, remind yourself of the great things in your life. A health crisis can be a nudge to push you towards living life to the full. If you have a friend who is unwell, buy them a really nice napkin holder, fill it with colourful napkins and tell them this story. A bunch of flowers is a colourful gift, but flowers only last a few days, whereas napkins are a reminder at every mealtime, every day that things will work out in the most AMAZING way.

People often expect doctors to have all the answers and to be able to provide them with a magic pill to take away all their illness and worries. In reality, you need to do some of the work yourself. Many symptoms can be caused by stress and anxiety, including stress headaches, poor sleep and various aches and pains. Always consult your doctor/nutritionist, but be open to trying different relaxation techniques and make sure that your diet and lifestyle support good health.

Most employers do little to invest in their employees' wellbeing, so it is up to you to keep as well as you can and to deal regularly with work pressures. Hypnotherapy recordings offer affordable solutions – you can listen to them at bedtime as you fall asleep. Hypnotherapy can help change bad eating, drinking and smoking habits as well as tackling stress and disrupted sleep, which will directly affect your physical health. As you start to feel more relaxed, you will be able to think of solutions rather than getting caught up in negative thinking.

Create boundaries in your life to support your health, limit the time you spend with people who drain you, limit your working hours, and switch your mind off from work in your spare time.

• Spend a couple of minutes every day SMILING and saying to yourself, 'I have an AMAZINGLY healthy body.'

If you are unwell and can't find out what is wrong with you because there is no clear diagnosis, do everything described above to make yourself as positive and relaxed as possible. Then use your energy to keep going until you do get a diagnosis. I tell all my clients the same thing: keep going until you find out what is wrong. By believing in the AMAZING outcome, you will be in the right place at the right time to get the best diagnosis and treatments available. But it is also important to do everything you can to look after yourself.

Health is not just a black-and-white issue: 'I am ill so that is that,' or 'I have this illness and there is nothing I can do.' There is always something you can do. Remember the grey area where the solutions for change are. Even if you are too ill to get out of bed, you can use positive mind techniques to stay calm. When you are calm, your body can use its energy for healing. When you are angry, everything seems much worse, both physically and psychologically.

Think of all the things you could do to help yourself and visualize yourself well. Learn to stand up for yourself to get what you need from health professionals. Do your own research. If doctors are unable to help you, you could suggest ideas to them that might open a new avenue of investigation. Your body is complex and there could be something that has been overlooked.

I was very ill after my daughter was born in 1992. I had so many symptoms, aches and pains, as well as fatigue and brain fog. I was housebound and at times struggled even to pick up my daughter. The doctors could not work out what was wrong with me. But I knew there must be a solution to my problems, and I was determined to find it.

Eventually, after two and a half years, it was discovered that I had a severe hormone imbalance. I was given a new hormone treatment and within five weeks my symptoms had resolved. Once I was well, when I met friends in the street or went into local shops with my daughter, she would tell people, 'Mummy doesn't sleep in the afternoon any more.' It was a complete revelation to her to see me well, because she had lived through the illness too.

So remember that you are not just getting better for yourself. You are also doing it for the people who love and depend on you.

Keep in the positive

'I can get through this. I am getting through this. I am doing it.'

SMILE and keep reminding yourself that it's all working out AMAZINGLY well. Turn your experience into something AMAZING. Try to enjoy what you can about this phase of your life. For me, even though it was a physically tough time, the AMAZING part of it was the time I spent at home with my daughter when I was unwell: if I had been well, I may not have taken time off work to be with her.

Medicine is evolving all the time, so a new test or treatment may soon be available. Every day, people all over the world are getting better. Find the positive in where you are with your health.

I had a client who hobbled into my clinic one day and was barely able to sit down. He had a bad back, arthritis and was drinking too much alcohol. 'I am old and I just have to accept it,' he told me. In fact, he was hypnotizing himself with doom and gloom and I knew that, once he changed his state of mind, he would feel better.

I used hypnotherapy to relax him, make him feel fitter and allow his mind to be solution-focused. On the day of a follow-up appointment, I looked out of the clinic window and saw him skipping along with a spring in his step. When he bounced into the room, he said that he had started using therapeutic magnets to improve the symptoms of the arthritis, had reduced his drinking and was feeling much better. He had a positive frame of mind and was like a man 20 years younger.

There are two important factors related to ill-health: one is the physical illness itself and the other is the need to deal with the stress and the impact it has on your life.

Hypnotherapy recordings are an excellent tool to help you release the stress and counterbalance the negative effects of health issues. Hypnotherapy is also useful in helping to prevent stress-related health issues. You can't control everything, but you can embrace things that may help.

Be open to making lots of small changes that will help you manage your health issues, get better and stay well. Remember, 1% better, then 10% better and before you know it you will be 50% better. You can use the percentage rule in other areas of your life too, to help you to find solutions and reach your goals.

The Internet is full of health information which, used sensibly in conjunction with a **supportive doctor**, can provide you with answers to your health-related questions in a way that would have been impossible just a decade ago. Look for solutions to improve your health.

Help other people who are ill

Be supportive and kind to people who are ill. Encourage them to find solutions. Remind them, 'It will work out AMAZINGLY well,' and 'Good things can come from any situation.' Remember that when someone is ill or in pain, it can be hard to be positive. Be patient with them – and with yourself if you are the person who is unwell. Although most people will be open to help, not everyone will want to take on board the suggestions you may make. Sometimes, people just want to do things their own way, which is something that needs to be respected.

If an illness is taking over your life, imagine putting it into a red triangle in your mind and shrinking it down to make it smaller. Visualize yourself doing the hobbies you love or would like to do. Believe that there is a way back to good health and financial independence. When you believe there is a way through your health issue, you will find a better way to move forwards to the best health you can have. Imagine a wiggly string leading you to the answers you need.

People may judge you as a hypochondriac, but don't take it personally: they probably haven't ever been ill, except for having a cold or flu, and they don't really understand what you are going through. But there are other people going through the same experience somewhere in the world. So don't feel alone. Turn the situation into something positive so that one day you will be able to share your knowledge to help someone else. (You might share your story, share information online, or just have a conversation with someone that helps them.)

Music control-settings technique

Imagine your mind and your life being like a music technician's control panel in a recording studio, with sliding buttons and switches that flick on and off. Imagine all those different control settings now, as you think about your health or the health of a family member or friend. Go to the health part of the control panel and slide the settings up and down as you imagine things working out in the best way. Move the sliders as you feel good about positive changes taking place. Adjust the settings as you feel good about your life becoming harmonious.

As the settings adjust, glide the slider buttons in different ways and switch off some of them if you want. Just do what feels right in your own creative way. Small adjustments create new choices and decisions. By tweaking the settings slightly here and there, you will tweak your attitude towards health and find solutions. It's like having a massage in your mind and a massage in your life to make you feel better. Close your eyes if you want to.

- You are an individual, so find the best solutions for YOU to live the longest, happiest life possible.

Take responsibility

The UK has a wonderful free National Health Service for everyone. It's AMAZING, but it does make people more reliant on solutions being provided for them rather than looking for those solutions themselves. If something is not offered on the NHS, be prepared to invest time and money in getting better. Living a healthy, happy lifestyle is the best place to start taking responsibility.

Listen to your body

Be realistic with your health limitations. For example, don't fly halfway around the world if it is going to compromise your health. Instead, do something more local. When you are not well, you have to learn to accept the fact that your plans may have to change. If people around you cause you stress, listen to your body. Depending on how it is reacting to certain situations and people, you may need to change your interaction with them or avoid them. Show respect for your body in the way you live your life. Do a job that suits your body and keeps you as well as you can be. You may need to adjust your career to suit your health.

Think positively

Focus on things you want to happen. SMILE and feel AMAZING. Imagine you are fit and well, running or playing tennis and, above all, that you are happy in your life: 'My health is AMAZING. My body is AMAZING.'

Value your life and the lives of other people. Don't wait for people to get ill before you appreciate them.

Cut the health hazards from your life and feel AMAZING.

Chapter summary

✂ Have colourful napkins every day to remind you to enjoy the moment.

✂ Use the wave technique: flow with your health like the waves flow in and out from the shore.

✂ Remember the percentage rule: all the small things that help will add up to you getting better.

✂ Keep focused to get the correct diagnosis and treatments.

✂ Use the music control-settings technique: adjust the settings so you feel good about your health becoming harmonious.

✂ Make yourself as calm and comfortable as you can be to help your health.

✂ Adjust your lifestyle to support good health.

STEP 1. Look after yourself.

STEP 2. Say 'AMAZING health'.

STEP 3. Be as well as you can be.

Identify the stresses and emotions that fuel your addictions. Then deal with them and set yourself free.

CHAPTER 13

ADDICTIONS AND
OBSESSIONS

Taking back control

You or someone you know may be affected by addictive behaviour. In this chapter I give tips and advice on the following topics:

Alcohol	Pornography
Anti-ageing	Shopping
Body image	Smoking
Drugs	Stress and anxiety
Food	Technology, social media and phones
Gambling	
Gaming	Theft
Gossip	Work

Anything we spend a lot of time doing will eventually become part of who we are. Once we've become that person, we will have to spend time reprogramming ourselves to learn different behaviour in order to break the bad habit. It is YOU and only you who can make the change, either alone or with support.

Everyone at some point has addictive behaviour or a weakness for something. I suggest that you accept this fact and then work out what you need to do to take control of whatever your weakness or addiction might be. You are an individual, so you need to do what is right for you. But don't close your mind to solutions that other people have found helpful. You never know: what has helped someone else might be right for you, too.

You need to focus on making changes that will break the bad habit. Do the following experiment to prove to yourself that it is possible to adapt to something new.

Move the rubbish bin in your kitchen. For a while, you will keep going back to the old place, but before long you will get used to the bin being somewhere else and will go to it automatically, without having to think about it. It's the same thing with an addiction or bad habit that you want to change: you need to change the behaviour and do it over and over again until you get used to the new way of being. It works because you store the habit in your subconscious mind and, once you have reprogrammed yourself, it will become natural for you to behave in the new way.

- You invested time in learning the addictive behaviour. You need to spend time breaking the bad habits too.

Generally, people who become addicted think of the short-term rewards and not the long-term consequences of their actions. People who don't become addicted are aware of the consequences and decide to make better choices and decisions to avoid addiction.

Your choices and decisions = consequences.

- If you overeat, you will put on weight.

- If you drink regularly, you will, over time, become more dependent on alcohol.

- If you take drugs, you may become addicted.

- If you spend money you don't have, you will end up in debt.

- If you gamble, you will lose money.

- If you watch too much pornography, you will damage your relationship.

- If you spend too much time playing computer games, you will achieve less in life.

- If you overuse technology, it will overrun your life.

- If you smoke, you could shorten your life.

- If you overwork, you could burn yourself out and damage your relationships.

- If you steal repeatedly, you will probably get caught eventually.

People who have addictions live in a fantasy world, not in the real world of consequences. People who avoid addictions are able to see the consequences.

At the bottom of every addiction is a series of reasons why the person can't be without the thing they crave. Often, the addiction is based on childhood issues such as lack of attention or too much pressure from parents or schooling, plus low self-esteem, stress, rebellion, feeling trapped, lost or bored, filling time or escaping from pressure. Everyone has a different upbringing and everyone responds differently to events in their lives. In my hypnotherapy recordings, I heal the whole person by dealing with life issues in a general way. Once the subconscious mind feels more contented, the person feels calmer, happier and more relaxed. When you feel comfortable feelings, you don't need anything external – objects or behaviour – to make you feel complete.

I am not a big believer in bringing up the past in great detail, as it can be stressful, or even destructive. But it is important to identify the possible causes of addictive behaviour and then move the mind on from those events. It's important to let go of grudges or blame and to remember that every person you have ever met has been doing the best they could based on their own personality and beliefs. Hypnotherapy is a great tool to help move the mind on from past events and, by breaking bad habits that are lodged in the subconscious mind, you will be able to restore contented feelings.

I chose to become a hypnotherapist because it can make a real difference to someone's life very quickly. Through my hypnotherapy recordings, I have helped thousands of people break bad habits. Hypnotherapy fast-tracks the reprogramming of the mind so that it abandons negative habits and creates positive, good habits. Recordings are a great way of doing that, as you can listen to them in the privacy of your own home, maybe putting them on at bedtime to enhance the quality of your sleep, they are very cost-effective, and you can work through a series of titles to help various areas of your life.

Most people don't know exactly what hypnotherapy is. The best way to find out is to experience it for yourself. I tried it during a period of stress in my life and discovered first-hand just how AMAZING it is. It was this positive experience that inspired me to train as a hypnotherapist, which was one of the best decisions I have made in my life so far. For most people, hypnotherapy is a quick and easy way to release the mind from cravings, break bad habits and at the same time deal with the emotions and stress that might be at the root of any negative addiction. The positive messages that are dripped into your subconscious mind during hypnotherapy become a reassuring background voice when you are finding it hard to be positive in your daily life.

Your life is creating your addictions

Identify the stresses in your life that make you drink, smoke, overeat, gamble... Then work to eliminate those problems from your life. Many people say, 'I don't have any problems. I just like drinking/eating/taking drugs.' But there is always something fuelling an addiction.

You can put out the fire, but if you don't fix the electrical fault, fire will break out again. Work at fixing the electrical wiring in your life and in your mind by making changes that will create a different reality. Address the problems in your life and change the way you react to them. Feel AMAZING and imagine things working out well. Don't allow yourself to be absorbed in things repetitively without making conscious decisions and setting boundaries. Identify what aspect of your life is pushing the buttons and causing you to behave addictively.

As well as looking at yourself, look at other people and learn from them. Analyse their behaviour and try to work out why they have their addictions. Do they lack confidence? Do they suffer from stress or have bad relationships? Do they feel bad about their life in some way? Are they hurting because of things that have happened in the past? Have they been surrounded by people with a particular behaviour for so long they can't see that there is another way?

Whatever you have achieved in your life so far, take time to see the difference you have made to other people. For society to function, everyone is reliant on everyone else, and your role is as important as anyone else's. Everyone and everything has a purpose, so feel good about yourself. If you are not happy with your achievements or with your life so far, use the techniques in this book to steer yourself in a new and better direction.

Everyone has special gifts and talents. You may already be doing a job you are really good at, but you may not see who you really are. Or you may be looking for a career change, be a stay-at-home parent or retired. Whoever you are, you should feel good about you. If you don't, there are answers and solutions that will help you. You just need to go out and find them and then grasp the opportunities they offer.

To get a different result, you need to do something different. Start today. This week, do things differently from the way you did them last week: buy different foods, avoid places where there are drugs or alcohol, go to a café not a pub, drive a different route to avoid the betting shop, change whatever you can to get the result you want. There is a whole new world out there that is different from the one you are used to. Go out and find it.

Feeling-good technique

Problem: I am feeling useless because I can't stop my addictive behaviour. What is wrong with me?

Answer: It's not great to feel like that, but it will pass. Repeat to yourself, 'I can be in control. I am in control. I make healthy choices.' Visualize all the times you have been in control and build upon these images in your mind. See your future with you in control. Visualize a wiggly string leading you to a life that's under your control. SMILE as you think of making good choices and decisions from now onwards.

Alcohol

There really is more to life than just drinking. Go out and find an AMAZING life that does not rely on alcohol. Use the SMILE technique so that you feel better about your day and inspired to build an AMAZING life.

Throughout your life you may have been programmed by people drinking around you, by television programmes, adverts or living in a culture of drinking that has normalized it in your mind. Remember that there are people in every country in the world who drink very little and still have a good time.

What is normal drinking? Normal drinking is having the occasional drink in the company of other people with a 'take it or leave it' attitude. If you are using alcohol to help you relax or are relying on it in any way, try to find other, non-alcohol-related ways of relaxing and enjoying yourself so that your drinking doesn't end up getting out of control. If you have started to count alcohol units, you are already drinking too much. Just have a couple of drinks occasionally. Sort out every area of your life by making new, better choices and decisions.

I recommend listening to hypnotherapy recordings at bedtime to break drinking habits and also to help release emotional stress so that you feel relaxed and sleep better. You can listen to other titles of hypnotherapy recordings as well, such as 'Confidence' and 'Relaxation', which will boost your positive feelings about yourself. When you are naturally relaxed, you won't feel the need for a drink.

- Take a shower or have a bath after work to relax you.

- Change into some comfortable clothes when you finish your working day.

- Drink herbal tea in the evening.

- Drink sparkling water in a wine glass with a slice of lemon instead of alcohol.

- Listen to hypnotherapy recordings after work or at bedtime.

- Use the techniques in this book to change your life for the better.

Take the b out of *booze* **and** *ooze* **personality without alcohol.** Be the life and soul of the party without a drink. Work on your confidence so that you don't feel you need to have a drink to enjoy yourself.

Visualize-your-life-positive technique

Let go of the negative film in your mind of you being 'the drunk'. Instead, visualize yourself doing healthy things with your time, such as going to the theatre, sailing, running, watching movies, reading books... It's your choice. Imagine yourself going through your week without alcohol.

Photo drink diary

Use your phone camera to make a photo drink diary by photographing everything you drink (alcoholic and non-alcoholic). This way you will really see what you are consuming. Share the pictures with a supportive friend so that you have to face up to what you are drinking. Eventually, your photo drink diary will include mainly non-alcoholic drinks, with the occasional drink of alcohol.

SMILE as you think about being happy without a drink.

Living with a drinker

If you live with a heavy drinker or an alcoholic, they might love drinking more than they love life itself. But most people who drink would like to be more in control of their lives, so the chances are that they will want to change. Photograph or film their behaviour so that you can sit down and present them calmly with the facts. Explain what it is like to live with them. Suggest that they listen regularly to an alcohol-reduction hypnotherapy recording. You could play the hypnotherapy recording in the background when they are drunk so that, over time, the messages filter into their subconscious mind.

I strongly suggest that you also work on yourself by listening to confidence-boosting and relaxation hypnotherapy recordings. These will help you to break any negative habits that have become established in your interactions with the person who drinks and will give you the confidence to be able to stand up for yourself.

Imagine things working out AMAZINGLY well whether or not you continue to live together.

Anti-ageing

Look at a photograph of yourself taken 10 years ago and see how fabulous you looked back then. In another 10 years from now, you will look back and think, 'What was I worrying about 10 years ago?' Today is the day for loving who you are and how you look. Start just being you, at the age you are, and accepting that this is who you are. Worrying about ageing is stressful and stress causes ageing. So stop getting stressed about the way you look. Instead, enjoy this phase of your life and feel AMAZING.

Do the best you can to eat well, sleep well, be relaxed and exercise sensibly and safely.

You may have brainwashed yourself into obsessing about ageing. Hypnotherapy can release the bad habits and help you to relax and feel good about yourself. Many of my clients look much younger after hypnotherapy sessions because we all carry life stresses in our faces and bodies. Also, hypnotherapy can help you to let go of bad eating or drinking habits so that your body can detox and repair.

Enjoy who you are and what you do in your life. Look after yourself so that you are healthy and youthful on the inside as well as on the outside.

SMILE, accept yourself and feel AMAZING.

Body image

Every 'body' is different. Yes, every single body out of all the billions of people in the world is completely different from every other body. Your body is part of who you are, so why would you want to change it? Love the body you have, really love it, appreciate everything it does for you and look after it.

Use hypnotherapy to feel confident about who you are. No one is perfect, so be the best you can be while being healthy. Don't buy into other people's expectations about looking a certain way. Instead, create your own unique look and style. Be naturally beautiful or handsome.

SMILE as you focus on the positives about the way you look.

Drugs

Be an individual and stop following the crowd. You may think that everyone takes drugs but that is because you surround yourself with other drug users. Of course, most people are not taking drugs. You need to change your life by finding things to do that do not involve drugs. Start doing new activities or hobbies that make your heart sing. For some people, that might involve something as simple as baking cakes or painting. Make new friends with people who have no connection with drugs or other drug users.

Ask yourself what is hurting inside you from your past that is making you feel the need to get high and why your everyday life is not fulfilling enough. Try to get high on good ideas and building a great life instead of on drugs. You can get off drugs, but you need to heal the inner part of you that is hurting. I recommend hypnotherapy to deal with inner confidence issues, heal your emotional past and retrain your mind to live a full, happy life.

Take the *d* out of *drug* and stop brushing your emotional problems and past pain under the *rug*. Face up to what your problems are. Start living drug-free because you love your life. Be strong, be confident, build a life you are excited to be living. Say, 'I can take control of my life. I can do it. I am doing it. It is done. I am creating an AMAZING life.'

SMILING creates positive chemicals in your brain, just like the drugs were doing. So switch your drug habit to SMILING because you are naturally happy.

If you live with a drug user, they might love drugs more than they love life itself. Imagine things working out AMAZINGLY well whether you remain with them or not. Work on yourself by listening to confidence-boosting hypnotherapy recordings, which will help break any negative habits that have built up between you and your partner, so that you can stand up for yourself.

Release drugs technique

Clasp your hands together and squeeze them tightly. Feel the strength you have. Imagine your body working well, your body clean and safe, your mind balanced. Now think of the most boring thing you can think of. It may be being bored in a lesson as a teenager, school homework, a long flight, listening to a dull speech, or whatever feels boring for you. Hold the thought in your mind and imagine it being 10 times more boring as you squeeze your hands together. Focus on the boring feeling. Now switch your thoughts to drugs and imagine they are boring, really boring. When you think about drugs you automatically feel bored by them. They are pointless and boring. After a moment, unclasp your hands. As you do so, you will feel that drugs are for other people and that you are ready to leave them behind. Release and relax your hands.

Food

The shops are filled with foods you don't need. To be slim, you need to eat regularly, small portions of wholesome foods with the occasional treat, and exercise regularly.

There is nothing else to it. You may feel that you don't like being on a diet, but a well-balanced diet is normal eating for slim people. There is no miracle cure, no magic pill or fad diet. You just need to learn to manage your eating. Find out what works best for you and stick to it. Accept the fact that to be slim you need to eat what your body requires, do the right amount of exercise and sleep well.

Whenever possible, eat fresh, home-cooked foods. Start by learning to cook one healthy recipe. Once you have mastered it, learn to make another recipe and then another, until you know so many recipes that the only food you cook is healthy food.

Hypnotherapy recordings used regularly will help to keep you in a positive frame of mind and keep cravings at bay. Say to yourself repeatedly, 'I can eat healthily. I can exercise and I am doing it. I am slim, fit and healthy.' Do not say, 'I am so fat.' Visualize yourself slim, fit and healthy. If you can't imagine that, stick a picture of your head on the photo of a slim body and put it in a photo frame somewhere you will see it regularly.

Photo food diary

Make a photo food diary by photographing everything you eat and drink so that you can really see what you are consuming. Maybe share the pictures with a supportive friend so that you have to face up to what you are eating.

Be the slimmest you can be. Do everything you can to make the best of you and your body. Dress in clothes that suit your body shape. SMILE, encourage and accept yourself.

Gambling

Your biggest assets are yourself and the money you generate each month. Let go of wasting time and money by gambling as you chase a financial dream. Instead, take control of your destiny by improving who you are and how much you can earn to provide for yourself and your family today and in the future. Start spending less and save all the money you would have spent on gambling in a special savings account. Use your time better: spend time retraining, analyse and adjust your finances to make savings, and increase your income. Invest time in finding out how you can invest your money safely.

Hypnotherapy will help you to let go of gambling habits, increase your wealth and create a better relationship with money.

Photo gambling-money diary

Take a photo of all the money you spend on gambling – cash, receipts, online transactions – so that you really see how your habit is affecting your finances. You may be shocked by how much you spend. Think about how you could use that money to invest for your future. Share the pictures with a supportive friend so that you have to face up to what you are doing.

Gaming

Gaming is a form of hypnosis: your mind is totally open and focused on the information you are receiving – by watching, in the case of gaming. Be aware of this, as the images and actions of the game are planting an impression in your mind that will eventually become part of your thinking. Gaming negative material could make you more aggressive and negative.

During one Christmas holiday break, I played a farm-game app to find out what it was like to be absorbed in a game. As well as finding it addictive, I dreamt about it and woke up in the morning with images and the music from the game playing in my head. I had been hypnotized within just three weeks.

The farm game was pretty positive, but a war game, for example, could be quite damaging. I chose to stop after completing the challenge, as I know how powerful hypnosis can be. Frankly, I would rather be doing something more positive and life-enhancing than looking at virtual chickens being fed. In fact, I wouldn't have written this book this year if I had continued to play the farm game.

A friend told me that she was called in for a meeting at the school her son attended, where all the parents of boy pupils were told that the boys were coming into school tired and unable to focus on their work because they were gaming, and that they were now lagging behind the girls. So gaming really is having an effect, which should not be taken lightly.

As well as kids gaming, some parents are doing it, too, instead of interacting with their kids, which means that there is very little conversation taking place in some households. Gaming just before going to bed is also a bad thing, as you will end up going to bed late and your sleep patterns will be disturbed because, instead of helping you to unwind, it will make you more alert. Find healthier ways to relax or limit the time you spend gaming. In my opinion, people who game are wasting time they could be using to build a great life and a financially secure future. Don't let your life pass you by.

SMILE and think of better ways to use your time. Hypno-therapy is a great tool to help reprogram you into having healthier habits again.

Gossip

Every word you speak shapes your life. If you spend hours talking about other people's problems or buying into negative dramas, your life will become a soap opera. Focus on your own problems and sort them out instead of talking about other people's. If you gossip, your life will become stuck in a negative pattern. If you are pleased for other people and share good news about them, your own life will flourish and get better.

Be kind and supportive to other people. Every day, say something positive about someone else. SMILE as you think about the good in other people.

Bad news junkie

Watch your words. Are you the one who shares the bad news? Do you like bad news about other people because it makes you feel better about yourself? Do you love a good doom-and-gloom story to top up your rage about the bad news in the world? Try to notice when you are saying something negative and switch your conversation to positive stories.

Every day, tell someone some good news.

Pornography

Sexual images are everywhere in daily life, in magazines, on the television and in music videos. As a result, they become normalized in our subconscious minds because we are programmed by our surroundings. Watching pornography online has also become acceptable for many people, particularly because it is so easily accessible. But this impacts on our relationships.

When you make love to your partner, you feel attraction. Touch, smell and all your other senses are absorbed, which contributes to the closeness you share with your partner. When you watch pornography, you are allowing a sexual image to stimulate you rather than a one-to-one connection with a partner. The mind can become overloaded with imagery and sexual expectation so that you become addicted to the reward in the same way you would become addicted to substances that create good chemicals in the body.

Pornography and relationships

A healthy relationship requires both parties to engage with each other. Anything that distances you will damage your relationship. Watching pornography behind your partner's back will not contribute to a healthy, happy, long-term relationship, because your partner may find out what you are doing and feel betrayed.

I knew a couple who were not living together in the week and who found that they were drifting apart. The woman was sexually excited to see her partner at the weekends, but he was less interested. They eventually realized that whereas she looked forward to being intimate with him at the weekends, he was watching pornography while he was away so was not as excited to see her. After talking it through, he decided not to watch pornography during the week and their sex life improved again.

If your partner is open to watching pornography with you occasionally, you may do this together. But be sensitive and do not put pressure on them, as they need to feel comfortable and watching pornography isn't for everyone. What's important is having fun with your partner, laughing together and being close. Romance your partner and make them feel special.

If you watch pornography on your own, you are only developing the visual image of sex in your mind, not the ability to have a healthy physical relationship with a partner. It may hamper you from getting out there and finding a healthy relationship, and when you do find someone you want to go out with, you may have unrealistic expectations of how they should look and perform sexually. You may have a distorted view of what is normal and acceptable in a sexual relationship with your partner. When you meet a partner, they are unlikely to find your pornography habits attractive. Romance is essential for a happy, balanced relationship and pornography can stop you making an effort to be romantic because you want instant results.

Red triangle technique

Imagine a red triangle in your mind. Imagine putting all the pornography you have watched in the past into the red triangle and then shrink the shape down in your mind. Repeat this technique several times to help reprogram your mind. Imagine having a healthy, happy relationship with your partner.

- Wean yourself off images.

- Use hypnotherapy recordings to break the habit of your pornography addiction.

- Make a conscious effort to connect with your partner.

- Focus on the feeling of being with your partner in a loving relationship.

- Create a happy relationship in which sex is part of your life, not the only focus.

- Read the chapter on relationships (Chapter 9).

Shopping

The shops are filled with beautiful items and AMAZING designs. There will always be something you want to buy. But you can't always have new things. Accept this, make the most of what you do have, enjoy looking at all the lovely items on sale, but leave them in the shops.

- Set yourself a budget of what you can spend each year and split it between the seasons.

- Use your money wisely.

- It takes a lot of time and effort to earn money and only a few minutes to spend it, so think about what you are doing.

- Appreciate what you already have.

- Sell items you no longer want.

- Never buy on credit. If you can't afford it today, you can't afford it – full stop.

- Keep track of everything you are spending.

- Spend less than you earn.

- Remember that there are people who have less than you have.

SMILE about what you have already.

Spending money

Getting caught up in an addictive spiral of spending money you don't have is no different from having any other kind of addiction. Be prepared to hear the truth about what you are doing. Your spending is your responsibility. Don't be selfish and expect other people to pick up the pieces when you overspend. You have to accept that if you can't afford items, you can't have them. Learn to budget and save up for the things you want. Remember that the amount of money coming in needs to be more than the amount you spend.

SMILE as you think about being debt free and then follow the steps described in Chapter 7 to become debt free.

Smoking

When you are really positive and living a good life, smoking will not be part of that life, as it goes against the grain of healthy, happy living. Smoking is masking your real inner feelings. Smoking suppresses your true emotions so that you can cope with daily life. When there is a crisis, smokers go straight outside to light up, whereas non-smokers can process the stress without a cigarette.

You may want to believe that it is just a chemical addiction, but smoking is also an escape from what has happened or is happening in your life. Learn to deal with your stresses and emotions without a cigarette. Little by little, change your life and then let go of smoking. Giving up smoking will enhance your life in every way, but it is important to sort yourself out first, otherwise you could pick up another bad habit to try to cope with stress, such as drinking or eating more.

For most smokers, hypnotherapy is a great tool for saying goodbye to cigarettes, cravings and emotional issues. You may need to go for a few sessions, but the money you invest in giving up is money well spent. You won't know whether it will work for you unless you try it.

Goals

Set yourself a positive goal that you will only achieve if you're fit, such as training to run a marathon, doing a charity run or going on a hill-walking or biking holiday. That way, there will be a real purpose to stopping smoking.

Photo cigarette diary

Use your phone camera to make a photo cigarette diary by photographing everything you smoke so that you really see how much you are smoking. I suggest taking a picture of each cigarette before you smoke it and then another of the butt after it is smoked. Share the pictures with a supportive friend so that you have to face up to what you are doing.

SMILE throughout your day to create positive feelings and think of all the things you will be able to do with the time you used to spend smoking.

Stress and anxiety

Could you be doing too much so that feeling stressed is a way of life and you have become addicted to it? Or do you tend to over-think everything so that you become worried about things you don't need to worry about?

Any time you notice yourself worrying about something, talk yourself into the positive as if you were reassuring a friend. Speak to yourself about how you would like things to work out. Tell yourself, 'It will work out AMAZINGLY well.' Rub, press or tap the knuckles on your left hand with the fingers of your right hand and imagine the problem passing like a cloud in the sky as you say the words, 'Let it pass.' (There are more tips in Chapter 3 about how to let go of worries.)

SMILE and think of the times when things worked out well.

Technology, social media and phones

Limit your use of technology, social media and phones. If you don't, using them could take over your life, affect your relationships and stop you reaching your true potential. See technology as a tool to help you in your life, but don't allow it to *become* your life.

I was on a train recently when a young woman phoned her boyfriend and told him all about her day, every detail from the moment she left home until she got on the train. She told him about a jacket she had bought, explaining why she bought that one and not another one, and then she said, 'Okay, well I have to go now. I'm getting off the train. I'll see you in a minute, outside the station.' The whole carriage had heard all the details of her life because she couldn't wait until she could talk to her boyfriend in person.

- Never use technology rather than talking to the people around you.

- Be balanced with your use of technology. Be aware that the overuse of technology can cause arguments.

- Make an agreement with friends to turn off your phones so that you can have meaningful conversations.

- Wait until you see people in person to tell them your news.

- Avoid being obsessed about getting in contact with people.

- Avoid constantly checking the news and social media.

- If you are in the company of someone when your phone rings, don't automatically answer it. Respect the person you are talking to.

- Switch your phone to 'flight mode' before you go into the bedroom. Your alarm will still ring, but you won't be disturbed by messages, alerts or radiation from the device.

- Avoid watching television or using technology in your bedroom.

- The last thing you hear before you go to sleep will be in your mind, so make sure it is positive. Perhaps play calming music at bedtime.

- Hypnotherapy can help reprogram your bad habits.

SMILE so that you are happy in everyday living. Instead of being absorbed by technology, notice your surroundings – the leaves on the trees, the sun shining – and the people around you.

Theft

Thieving is a bad habit, just like any other bad habit. Perhaps you want things that you can't see any other way of getting. Or you take things simply because they are there and because you can. Or you think you deserve the things you take. Or you think you'll be happier if you have a particular item. Or you think that the people you are taking something from can afford to lose it.

Once you see thieving as a habit, you can begin to change it by making different choices and decisions. For example, avoid going to places where you would have stolen things in the past. If you feel the items you want are out of your reach, you are thinking in the black-and-white zone, not the grey zone where solutions are found.

Instead of saying to yourself, 'I need to steal this item because I can't afford to buy it,' say, 'If I change my choices and decisions in life, I might find a way to live my life differently.'

Tell yourself, 'Maybe one day I could have these things'.

Instead of saying, 'I can't afford these things, but I can take them without getting caught,' say, 'I probably don't even need these things. Maybe I can become wealthier through making AMAZING choices and decisions to improve my life.'

Red triangle technique

Visualize a red triangle in your mind. Put the negative thoughts about wanting things that are not yours into the triangle, together with the problems and the behaviour.

Then shrink the triangle down in your mind until it is as small as a speck of dust and imagine blowing the speck of dust away. As the triangle dissolves, you will allow AMAZING solutions to reveal themselves to you over the coming days and weeks. Feel good about yourself for being in control of your choices and decisions. Repeat this exercise as many times as you want. Presume that good things will come from today and that people have good things to say about you.

'AMAZING things happen to me because I make good choices and decisions. I find AMAZINGLY positive ways to make my life go smoothly.'

Work

Try to break the habit of overworking by being aware that that's what you are doing. You may feel as though you are constantly chasing your tail because you believe that this is the only way to behave. Start believing that you can be successful and be calm and relaxed. Once you have made your mind aware that you are doing too much, you can start to come up with solutions to fix the problem. I suggest calming yourself down by just being aware at intervals throughout the day of being in your own body. Say to yourself, 'I get everything done in less time.'

Gradually work to take back control of the situation. Set boundaries, such as turning off your phone after work, and make time for family, friends and interests. Listen to calming relaxation music at bedtime and get a full night's sleep.

Techniques to help release addictions

Talk-to-a-photo technique

Find a photograph of yourself when you were happy. Look at the photo and tell yourself what you need to hear. Self-talk positively to yourself. What would you tell a friend? 'You are worth so much more than this. You can find a way to get out of this and stop this behaviour. You will find solutions. Start believing in yourself. You can do it. You are AMAZING. You can change what you need to change to create a great life. I am here for you. I will support you.' Repeat this exercise regularly to encourage yourself.

New music technique

Take a few minutes regularly in private to listen to positive music that feeds your soul. SMILE as you do this. You can also dance or move your body in a way that feels right for you. You don't need to follow any set pattern. Just feel free. Choose new, different styles of music rather than old favourites that might remind you of past events that may be linked to past addictive behaviour. From now onwards, it is about creating 'new' positive experiences.

Positive future technique

Train your mind to see positive future images of your great life without the addiction. Speak the words of the person you want to be. Be aware of who or what has helped you along the way. Appreciate every little step and keep moving forwards. If something helped you before, try it again. Build an armament of the things that help you. Focus, focus, focus and SMILE to create uplifting feelings.

Cut the root of the addiction, free yourself and feel AMAZING.

Chapter summary

✂ Visualize yourself living your life without the addiction.

✂ Say, 'I can be in control. I am in control. I make healthy choices.'

✂ Use the red triangle technique: put the addiction into a red triangle in your mind and shrink it down until it is like a speck of dust.

✂ Talk to a photo of yourself. Say, 'You can turn this into a positive. You can work through this. You can get over this.'

✂ Move freely to positive new music that makes your soul sing.

STEP 1. **Identify your problems.**

STEP 2. **Feel more positive about things working out AMAZINGLY well.**

STEP 3. **Change your lifestyle to create new habits that let go of your addiction.**

Life is a series of new beginnings.
Let the past heal and the future be even better.

CHAPTER 14

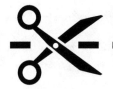

HEARTACHE, BEREAVEMENT, DIVORCE AND LOSS

Cut the pain from your life and feel AMAZING

Your whole life is a series of beginnings and endings, hellos and goodbyes. From the moment you are born into the world, people will come in and out of your life, either individually or in larger numbers, for example when you start nursery, go to school or leave home. You can choose to feel sad about the endings and goodbyes, or to embrace them as part of normal living and live each day to the full as if tomorrow and every day that follows it is a new adventure.

If you have experienced some kind of loss, you may be feeling devastated and believe that you will never really enjoy life again. It's true that life will be different, but there is no reason why you can't eventually replace the pain you have experienced with joy. There is an old saying that time is a great healer. But it is not time itself that heals you, it is what you choose to do with it. If you tell yourself that you will find ways to make your life wonderful, even better than it was before, your mind will become solution-focused and open to the things that will help you.

Stepping-stone technique

Accept the way you feel and that it may take some time to release all your emotions. Give yourself the space and time you need and then imagine all those feelings are part of the path of your life. See the event that has occurred as a stepping stone in a long line of stepping stones in your past and know that you will create more stepping stones in the future. Every time you think of the person or event, see it as a stepping stone rather than as a movie running repeatedly in your mind. By taking control and stopping the movie of past events, you will get out of the emotional spiral. Imagine there is a wiggly string in front of you leading you to everything you need to be able to accept and move on from your loss or bereavement.

- If you feel a bereavement feeling, sit with it and let it pass as you say, 'It is working out AMAZINGLY well.'

Good can come from every situation and you need to get up each day ready to find the good that is out there for you. Once you find the good that will help you, you will be able to use your own knowledge and experience to help someone else one day. Remember, you are not alone. There is a lot of loss in the world – it is part of life.

There is nothing you can do to change the past, but you can change the way you feel about the past so that you can move forwards to your future. Be happy for the good times you experienced. Be contented. Find the lessons to be learned from what has happened. And remember that everyone else is creating their own life, just like you must create your new life going forwards.

If you have suffered an injustice, remember that everyone is doing the best they can. Everyone has limitations, so try to accept them for who they are or were. Assume that whatever has happened was meant to happen, and allow yourself to live a better life.

We are programmed from a young age to believe that everything should be perfect, whereas in reality we are all part of nature and life can be unpredictable. If your subconscious mind was taught from a young age that loss and bereavement may happen and if certain events do occur you will feel fine, you would probably cope easily when they did. But it's more likely you were told that life is supposed to be a certain way and it didn't work out that way when you experienced loss. You are a sensitive and loving person, and you are also strong enough to get through what has happened. You can, you will and you are already getting through it. Try the following exercise to help you.

Happy photo technique

Find a happy photo of yourself and the person you have lost.

1. Speak to the image of yourself. Tell yourself whatever you want to say. Let the emotions out. Say the sad things, say the good things, cry unhappy tears and cry good tears. Let the sad feelings release to allow the happy feelings to flow again. Tell yourself you can be happy again. Tell yourself you will find happiness again. Don't let other people spoil your happiness. Speak to yourself as you would if you were reassuring a small child. Say, 'Things will work out AMAZINGLY well. Your life will be even better. You will find a way to make this whole episode work out as well as it can.'

2. Speak to the image of the person you have lost. Tell them everything you want to say. Tell yourself, 'My life without you is going to be an AMAZING adventure. I will prove to you that my life will be AMAZING.'

Changing seasons technique

We are all part of nature and, just like nature, life is a series of seasons: the flowers begin to open in the spring; in the summer they blossom some more; in the autumn the leaves fall from the trees; and in the winter the cold days allow us to appreciate the warmth of our homes. Without the heat, you would not understand the cold. Without the rain, you would not notice the sun. Like nature, your life is a continuous journey of change. Some of those changes will involve personal difficulties that will teach you things, such as compassion and kindness to others. There will always be changes in life. Learn from your experience of loss never to allow change to affect you so much that it causes you pain. Life is too precious to allow it to be interrupted so abruptly by hurt. Let it dissolve. There is good in every situation. Learn to flow with what is happening. Breathe calmly and deeply and feel relaxed about the situation as you think of the seasons changing and life flowing again from now onwards.

A few years ago, I lost a dear, close friend to cancer. I decided I would not let her loss be a painful experience. So, in honour of her, I put nice napkins on the table every day (no more waiting for birthdays and special occasions). Using a nice napkin is a reminder to me to live every day to the full and to have an AMAZING life. It also helped me to feel more positive when I thought about my friend. Paper napkins have a positive, uplifting feeling as they are associated with celebrations and so they remind you of good times.

One day, my sister visited and commented how nice it was that I had a pile of brightly coloured patterned napkins in a napkin holder on the table. 'What are we waiting for?' I asked her. 'I mean, really, what are we waiting for? Let's start living!'

'You are so right,' my sister said. 'I am going to start having pretty napkins every day too!'

Even in a restaurant when I am offered a napkin, I SMILE to myself, as it reminds me to be happy. The napkin is just a symbol of the need to appreciate life.

Buy a napkin holder, fill it with colourful paper napkins and start living each day. (And, please send me a picture of your napkins: Ailsa Frank blog, Twitter @AilsaFrank or Instagram ailsafrank)

- There really is no time like the present.

- Find purpose to your life again.

- Make your daily living a happy experience.

Remember, before you lost the person, you were getting on with the majority of your day or your week independently from them. You will gradually get used to being independent and without them all of the time. Focus on getting through the next minute or hour or day or week. Take it step by step, but keep moving forwards.

- If you have lost a pet, get another one.
- If you have been betrayed, find a better partner.
- If you have lost a loved one, find hobbies, a career and people to help fill the gap.
- If you have lost a child, find purpose in your life by doing something AMAZING.
- Do something special to replace the loss.
- Turn the situation into something AMAZING.

The plan has changed. You can cope with the new plan, so start feeling excited about it. It's normal to have a bad moment. Let the feelings pass like clouds in the sky. Make plans and enjoy the adventures ahead. There will always be something positive to help fill the empty space left in your life when you lose someone. It will be different, but it can be good.

Getting over the heartache of divorce or a break-up

Men and women can be equally distressed over a divorce. It is common to feel frustration and upset. A client had a lot of anger towards her ex-husband because he had run off with another woman. After sessions with me, she started to see that the relationship had actually broken down over time. She realized that she had sometimes been unreasonable too – she had not always been open to discussions and she was seeing things as black and white – and maybe that was partly why he left, because there was no room for negotiation. She also accepted the fact that because her ex-husband was still helping to support her financially, she didn't have any money worries. She started to be more grateful for his financial support instead of feeling resentful. Eventually, her anger dissolved and she became friends with her ex-husband, which made life very much better for the children. When she came to terms with him being with someone else, she was able to move on with her life. And then she met someone else too, having learned from the experience.

- **Accepting things have turned out the way they have will help dissolve stress and hurt.**

If you have lost children in a divorce situation, you need to keep up your contact with them, let them know you love them and do something AMAZING with your life to fill the void. Remember, children will grow up and one day things might change and you could be close to them again.

We have all been brought up with fairytales that tell us there is one prince or princess out there for us and that, once we are together, we will live happily ever after. In reality, there are many princes and princesses, none of whom is totally perfect. You will find someone else and when you do, you will be able to use the experience from the past to get things right, by being reasonable, communicating well with that person and working through things together.

You will get over the relationship break-up you have been through and you will move on. There are millions of people in the world and I assure you that there is someone out there for you. There is never just one person who is right for you. So believe that someone even better will come into your life.

The following tips will help you.

1. See the relationship as a stepping stone in your journey of life. See it as being behind you, as part of the path leading you to a great relationship. Whenever your ex-partner pops into your head, see the stepping stone.

2. If that person had been right for you, things would have worked out. Say to yourself, 'I am AMAZING and I deserve to be with someone who treats me well.'

3. Say to yourself, 'It's all working out AMAZINGLY well.' No matter what is going on, presume that it will all work out AMAZINGLY well and that your life will get even better than it could have been if you had remained with that person.

4. Work on yourself. The more happy and confident you are, the more likely you are to meet someone who respects you.

5. Never allow others to take away your happiness. Go out and create new happiness by doing things you love. Learn something in a class or do something else AMAZING so that you can look back at this time as being the time when you made your life even better.

6. Love everyone, even if you don't see eye to eye with them. See the funny side of everyone and everything. Learn to laugh at yourself and at the world. Everyone is doing the best they can.

7. Get out of black-and-white, rigid thinking, such as, 'This has happened, so it's all rubbish now.' Instead, start living in the grey area, which is where the solutions are. Live in a world that is filled with possibilities. Say, 'This has happened, but I can and I will turn it into something good.'

Read this chapter regularly until you feel better.

SMILE, SMILE, SMILE at all the good things about the people who have touched your life. It will all work out AMAZINGLY well if you let it.

Cut the sadness and feel AMAZING.

Chapter summary

✂ Do new, interesting things you didn't do before your loss.

✂ Imagine a wiggly string leading you to everything you need to make a full recovery from the events.

✂ Use the happy photo technique: speak to a photograph of yourself, tell yourself what you are feeling, let the emotions out and then tell yourself it will all work out AMAZINGLY well. Tell a photo of the person you lost that you will make your life an AMAZING adventure.

✂ Build a positive routine of looking after yourself.

✂ Have colourful paper napkins at every meal to remind you to appreciate every moment.

✂ The plan has changed and you can cope with the new plan.

✂ Plan things to look forward to.

STEP 1. Accept that the events have happened.

STEP 2. Understand that you will feel fine again.

STEP 3. Allow the event to turn into something positive.

If you sit around waiting for it to happen, it won't.
But if you start living a life you love, you will feel
more contented and you will find a great partner.

CHAPTER 15

FINDING LOVE

There are millions of people in the country you are living in and there is definitely more than one person who is suitable for you. It is crazy to think that you will end up on your own. Of course you can find someone, in the same way you can make anything happen in your life. By making good choices and decisions, you can find, nurture and enjoy a good relationship. If you sit around waiting for it to happen, it won't. By living a life you love, your positivity will bring more happiness into your life and you will end up finding a great partner.

Do things you enjoy, look after yourself, build your confidence, make the best of your looks and feel AMAZING. Your positivity will catch the attention of a good partner for you. But instead of focusing on finding someone, start living each day and building the life you want. The more you are your true self, the more suitable your new partner will be, as you are quite likely to meet someone who is on the same level of positivity as you are. See this phase as a time to discover who you really are. Feel a confident feeling that it will all work out AMAZINGLY well, in the same way that other things in your life have worked out well for you.

You may be feeling that you can't move on from a past relationship. It is important to free yourself from past upsets and disappointments so that you can embrace a new relationship fully.

Moving-on-from-past-relationships technique

Read this regularly: My life is flowing and moving. There are solutions to everything. I need to be in the grey area, not in the black-and-white area. There is not just one way. There are many ways. It's okay to have a moment that is not so great. I can let the feeling pass like clouds in the sky. I can reassure myself using the knuckle-rubbing/pressing/

tapping technique, stroking my left knuckle with the fingers of my right hand until the feeling passes. I can see the way forwards as a wiggly string finding the solutions along the way. I can SMILE and let the good feelings flow again. Other people must have got over similar things. I can too. People do move on from these things all the time. The past was a foundation to prepare me for a great partner now. Life is an adventure. I can turn this experience into something AMAZING.

Improve who you are

Are you a great partner or are you demanding? Are you too giving? Are you needy? Do you lack confidence? Or are you so independent that you don't make time for anyone else or don't allow anyone into your life because you're afraid of them taking too much control? What were you told about relationships when you were growing up? Perhaps that it's best to be independent and that no one needs to have a partner?

Work out where you went wrong in your past relationships and how you could be different from now onwards. It is easy to blame the breakdown of a relationship on your ex-partner's behaviour. But if, for example, they bullied you, why did you not stand up for yourself? What can you do better this time around? What did you learn from your parents' relationship? Was it good or bad? What have you learned about relationships from your life experience so far? What can you do to make sure you get things right?

Hand on heart, you probably knew things weren't right in past relationships. Maybe you or your partner, or both of you, did not work through the problems. Make sure that this time, when you find a person with whom you could have a good long-term relationship, you find ways to work things out. But avoid overcompensating. For example, perhaps you were controlling in your past relationship and you think it contributed to the break-up, so you take a back seat in your new relationship and allow yourself to be bullied. It is common for people to go too far the other way instead of finding the middle ground and getting the balance right.

A client of mine had recently met a guy she really liked. They were having a lot of fun together, going to the cinema, for walks, for drinks in pub gardens and just hanging out at home watching TV. 'But he's just not my type,' she told me. 'He's a bit "normal" for me. I am not sure if I should get involved. I feel confused. I am used to going out with men who are more outgoing, party types.'

I told her that life is not just about partying and that she really needed someone she felt comfortable with in everyday life. And I reminded her that the cool, party-loving, good-looking guys she had known in the past had always ended up breaking her heart or using her. I suggested putting any decision about her new boyfriend on a shelf in her mind and revisiting it at a later date to allow her to get on with enjoying his company while the relationship developed.

It is a common issue I encounter with clients – they are worried to commit to someone because they think there might be someone better out there. But a happy, balanced, loving relationship is based on how you interact on a one-to-one level. I discussed this with my client and she realized that the old type of boyfriend was probably not right for her any more. She decided that she would keep seeing the new guy so that she could get to know him better and give the relationship a chance to develop. Sometime later, she told me that 'the new type' was definitely her thing, she was living happily with her boyfriend and they were planning to have a family together and that the work we had done had changed her life.

Although it isn't fair to mislead someone if you are not going to stay with them, sometimes you just need to give things a chance and allow yourself enough time and space to make the right decisions.

Shelve-it technique

Try to relax and let life be an adventure. If you don't know the answer to something today, don't worry about it. Just put it on a shelf in your mind and revisit it in a week, a month or six months. If you don't know the answer today, it may be that today is not the right day to make the decision. Shelve it, and always know that it will work out AMAZINGLY well.

If someone is not prepared to commit to you because they are in another relationship, move on. If you accept being second best, you will be treated that way. Ask yourself why you expect so little for yourself. Why would you want to prove that you can take someone else's partner? Tell them, 'This isn't good enough for me. I suggest you go back to your partner and sort your issues out. Thanks but no thanks. I have a life to get on with.' Walk away from time wasters. There will be someone AMAZING for you.

I have often heard clients say, 'All the good men/women are taken.' Then, a few weeks later, after some therapy sessions with me, they come back and tell me they have met someone really nice.

Negative

- If you say to yourself, 'All men/women are useless,' you will become involved with partners who are useless.

- If you say to yourself, 'All the good men/women are taken,' you won't meet a good man or woman.

- If you say to yourself, 'I can never settle with one person,' you will never settle with one person.

- If you say to yourself, 'I will be sad and alone forever,' you will be sad and alone forever.

Positive

- If you say to yourself, 'I am with an AMAZING, kind and caring man/woman,' you will be with that person.

- If you say to yourself, 'I am happily married and living in a beautiful home,' you will be living that life.

- If you say to yourself, 'I am a wonderful, considerate partner to my loving, considerate partner,' then you will have a loving relationship.

The truth is that both parties in a relationship need to be independent, to share time together, to be reasonable and to feel free in that relationship. If you think you should never have to change to be in a relationship, you are being inflexible, and good relationships are based on flexibility. You both need to adapt to be able to work well together.

Being complete

Whole circle technique

You were born into the world whole and complete like a perfect circle. Then, gradually, life chipped away at you until the circle became a bit wiggly and misshapen. If you were not your whole self, you probably attracted a partner who was a reflection of who you were. This partner, who you thought was perfect, was in fact a wiggly circle too, having been affected by life like you had. Visualize your circle of life being whole and perfectly round as you imagine you are back to your true self again.

To find the right partner, you need to get yourself back to your whole true self again by using the techniques in this book to improve your confidence and build a life you love. Then, once you know who you really are, you will meet someone who is on the same level of positivity as you are. You will be a whole, complete circle again, they will also be a whole, complete circle, and you will both be happy and confident. You will be grateful that any old relationships ended so that you were able to discover yourself and meet this new person. Your past break-ups have simply set you free.

Being flexible and open with each other is key to adapting to the way each of you does things. Often, people split up early on in a relationship because one party gets cold feet about committing. If that happens, don't worry about it. If a relationship is meant to be, it will happen. Set the other person free knowing that everything will work out AMAZINGLY whether you are with them or not. Sometimes, people need time to get used to the idea of being with someone and they will realize what they have lost when they are not with them any more. Allow the relationship to develop in its own time. If you are a woman, allow yourself to be courted: don't chase the man you are interested in or he will run a mile. If you are a man, be romantic, but know when to stop, particularly if you are getting a clear message that the woman you are interested in is not interested in you. It is about both sides getting the balance right.

Alcohol can make people do things they wouldn't dream of doing without a drink. So only ever have sex with someone you would have sex with when sober. And don't use sex to get attention from someone: there needs to be more to a relationship than attention-seeking sex.

'Getting the right property'

Think of dating as being like doing a property search. It is rare to buy or rent the first property you see. Most people have a good look around and view quite a few properties before deciding on the one that suits them best. Sometimes, people think they've found the right property and then the sale falls through and they are disappointed. But they always find a better one in the end. Enjoy the 'property search', but be ready to commit when the right one comes along. Enjoy dating and getting closer to your goal. You will find the right person for you. In the meantime, enjoy your single life while it lasts, knowing that love is on the way!

Single and looking for love – 'finding a comfy pair of shoes'

Another analogy I use is that a good relationship is a bit like a comfy pair of shoes that fit well and feel right, whereas a bad relationship is like shoes that aren't really comfy but you want them so much you buy them anyway. From the moment you buy the ill-fitting shoes, they cause you trouble. They give you blisters and swollen, sore feet, but you persevere because you invested so much in getting them that you can't just abandon them and let them go. Sometimes, you buy a pair of shoes that you are not entirely sure about but that end up being your favourite pair because they go with everything you ever want to wear.

Try to think of finding a partner as being like getting a good pair of shoes. Be honest with yourself and give the relationship time to see if it works out. But be prepared to let it go if it's really not comfortable and not the right thing for you.

Finding a great partner

If you want love right now, speak positively and make it happen. Be confident in yourself. SMILE and say to yourself, 'I am AMAZING. Of course someone is going to love me. I can have a great partner.' Tackle it as you would any other part of your life. Do what you need to do to make it happen. Go to places, join classes, be interesting, have a full life.

Think of things in your life that have worked out well and feel the same feeling as you think about having a partner. Start believing in a great relationship happening for you. Get yourself in the most positive place. When you are happy and contented, you will meet someone who you feel happy and contented with. Don't focus on preconceived expectations of who you want to be with. Instead, focus on the feeling of being with someone who is easy to get along with and compatible in each area of your life. Focus on love, happiness and having an AMAZING relationship.

- Marry and have children with someone who is a reasonable and decent person.

- A good relationship is all about getting the right balance and working well together.

Growing-old-happily-together technique

Imagine you and your wonderful (new) partner have grown old together. Imagine looking back over your life at all the things you have shared together, such as holidays, children, grandchildren or whatever you would like to have happened. Repeat this technique regularly. When you see other happy couples, SMILE and say, 'It's AMAZING. I have a lovely partner too.'

Self-talk yourself into the positive by saying, 'I am AMAZING. I am a great partner to be with. I love my AMAZING partner. I married well. It has all worked out AMAZINGLY well.'

Cut the waiting around for someone and make it happen AMAZINGLY.

Chapter summary

✂ Be whole and balanced so that you meet someone who is whole and balanced too.

✂ Use the shelve-it technique: if you can't make a decision, put the problem on a shelf in your mind.

✂ Give relationships a chance by getting to know people.

✂ Teach each other to know what you both like.

✂ Think of dating as doing a property search. You will find the right one in the end if you are open to what is realistic for you.

✂ Find a partner who is like a comfy pair of shoes that fit really well.

✂ Don't speak negatively about a date to friends. Focus on the positives.

STEP 1. Understand the past was part of your learning.

STEP 2. Make your life interesting.

STEP 3. Be open to a different type of relationship.

Take the good from your own childhood and then do a better job than your parents did.

CHAPTER 16

PARENTING

You are guiding your children by teaching them how the world works

Your parents, or whoever brought you up in their place, were the biggest influence on you and you are the biggest influence on your children. Good parenting is about balance. Take the good things from your own childhood, mix them with common sense and do a better job than your parents did.

It is common to overcompensate for a miserable childhood by swinging to the other end of the scale. For instance, the person whose parents were not interested in them may pay too much attention to their own children, causing them to feel trapped. Or perhaps your parents micro-managed your childhood, which annoyed you and made you too laid-back with your own children. If this did happen to you, you may not set boundaries and address behavioural issues because you want your children to feel free. But freedom needs to be balanced with structure and routine, which children enjoy too.

Rather than focusing on what your parents got wrong, I suggest that you look at the things they did right, as every parent does the best they can with the knowledge they have at the time. Even if you were not brought up by your own parents, maybe they did the best they could in the circumstances and with their abilities. Maybe it was better for you not to be with them. Or maybe what was done for you was the best that could be done by the people who had to make the decisions. Whatever your upbringing was like, it will have involved at least some things that made you a better person.

Remember some of the things your parents or carers got right, such as reading you stories, cooking for you, taking you swimming, teaching you to drive or cook, going on holiday, working to pay for things, giving you a home, or loving you in their own way. The next time a negative thought about them slips into your mind, switch your thoughts to something good that came out of your childhood.

Your job as a parent is to explain to your children why we do things, what the rules are and why we need to stick to them, so that they understand how the world works. If children are told to sit still and be quiet but they don't understand why, they will not learn to look for the reasoning in everything or to work things out for themselves. Always give a reason and an explanation when you ask your children to do something.

Rules need to make sense

I was out with a friend and her child one day. It was raining and we had just got off a boat on a river. It was a pretty miserable day and the child kept asking, 'Can I have an ice cream now?' Every time she asked, the mother said 'No.' After a while, the mother turned to me and asked, 'Can you do something, Ailsa?'

'We can't have ice cream because it's raining and it would be too cold to stand outside in the rain while we ate it,' I told the child. 'Let's go to a café instead, where it will be warm and dry.' The child said 'Okay' because it now made sense to her, and the mother then realized that explaining things to the child was better than simply saying 'No.'

'It's your job to explain everything to your child,' I told the mother. 'You are her teacher. She needs you to tell her how the world works.'

'I never really saw it that way,' the mother said. 'I just thought she was pestering me constantly, always going on about things.'

As a therapist, I have seen many parents trying to control every aspect of their children's lives. A typical comment is,

'We are so motivated and driven and we just want our child to be like us.' Some parents tell me that their children are not sticking to the mind map programme they have devised for them and that they complain about having to study every day during the school holidays. Sometimes they are talking about children as young as nine years old. Personally, I think all homework should be banned from school holidays so that children can have a complete break from all the stresses of school.

Remember, when you were a child, you did not have the drive and determination you may have now. You were just a child. So let your children be children too and don't expect them to think like adults. You can tell them that if they work hard, they will reap the rewards and that they need to find their special niche in life, because everyone has their own strengths. You can explain to them that we all need to stick to the rules and that doing their school work is important. But let them choose how they spend their spare time and let them do the hobbies that interest them.

If you want your children to be confident, let them do the activities they are good at, so that they can feel confident about what they are doing. There is no point sending them to martial arts classes intending to make them more confident if they hate being hurt during training sessions and have no interest at all in martial arts. Successful people can make it harder for their children by pushing them when they are too young and by setting goals that are too far out of their reach, so that they end up giving up anyway.

Causing stress to your children is a form of abuse

Life is stressful enough without parents adding pressure to the lives of their children. Children have to live with their parents until they grow up and can fend for themselves. For a child, living with a parent who causes them stress is like being an adult trapped in a stressful job from which you can't escape. Parents' obsessions – about their child being top of the class, the best sports player, the first in the class to read – can cause children the most extreme kind of stress. To deal with your own issues, I recommend listening to hypnotherapy recordings for parenting, which will help you to feel relaxed and communicate well with your children.

If your child wants to do design, for example, don't push them into medicine. If you do, you will set them off on the wrong path in life. Every choice and decision they make now will affect their future. So encourage them to build the life *they* want to live. If you don't allow them to be themselves, you will end up creating distance between you, as they will eventually break free and make their own choices without discussing things because they don't want you to control or influence their decisions.

I knew some parents who said they would only financially support their son, Chris, at university if he chose an academic subject. Chris found a degree in graphic design he wanted to do at a university at the other end of the country. His father said that it was too far from home and the course wasn't academic enough. So, acting against his own wishes, Chris went to a university nearer home to study law, just to keep his father happy. Soon after starting the degree, Chris signed up for a study year abroad without telling his parents. His decision caused a lot of arguments, because his parents were worried about him being so far from home. But he went on the study year and, in the end, his parents' manipulation backfired and caused a distance between them and their son.

- Deal with your own stresses so that you are calm.

- Adjust your life so that you are able to cope with your daily routines.

- Have healthy and realistic expectations of your children.

- Teach your children to follow their dreams.

- Trust in your children's ideas and choices.

- Remember that academic achievements are only a small part of the talents of any child.

- Allow your child to have a confident, outgoing personality, as this will take them far in life.

The ponds in life get bigger and bigger

At the crèche or nursery, it might be quite easy to be 'top of the class' because the pond is very small. Then the child goes to infant and junior school where, although there are more children in a bigger pond, it still might be fairly easy to be top of the class. When the child goes to senior school, the pond is even bigger and it becomes even more difficult to be the top student, although it may still be possible. Then, if they go to university or college, being the top student becomes harder still, as the pond is now filled with other top academic students. Once your child leaves education and enters the world of work or parenting, there is suddenly no such thing as the 'top person'.

There are so many people in the world and everyone has a place in making it function. The provision of every item and service we buy relies on a stream of people. Teach your children that everyone has a value and that they must find the best route for themselves in life. Letting go of the obsession for your child to be 'top of the class' will allow them to flourish and reach their own true potential, rather than being in a constant state of stress as they try to live up to your inflated expectations.

Your child's life will be AMAZING if you teach them to be themselves, work hard for themselves, develop their skills and find solutions, but also to be happy and relaxed. Teach them to work things out for themselves so that their mind develops the habit of doing it. If you keep sorting things out for them or making decisions for them, they could still rely on you to do the same thing when they are grown-up.

Say to your children, 'You will work things out. It will all sort out AMAZINGLY well.' Remind them of times when things worked out well.

If a teacher tells your child that they won't get to university, tell them that if they want to go they will find a way. Teach them that they *can* find a way. Teach them to imagine that they are finishing their degree and that they did everything they needed to do to get a degree, if that is what they want. It is up to us as individuals to carve out the life we want and it is your job to tell your children that they can make their life anything they want it to be. But let them find the way.

The workplace is changing rapidly and there are now industries that didn't exist 10 years ago. So don't let your limiting thinking stop your children finding the right career path. Let them make choices and decisions about their future that make sense for them. By the time they leave school, there may be even more new careers that you don't know about yet. When they show an interest in anything, it could be something that resonates with them for a career later.

- A teenager who spends more time looking at fashion magazines than studying may go on to run a fashion company.

- A computer geek who loves gaming may go on to be an IT expert.

It's all about balance. Obviously, you don't want your child to become addicted to gaming. But they may pick up some useful focus skills and an interest in computers if you encourage them to look deeper into their hobby by finding educational films on YouTube or other websites about how computer games are made, or how computers work and are built.

Don't make life a drama

Your children are mirror images of you. So if you are anxious about burglars breaking into the house, they will be too. If you are stressed about the traffic, your children will be too. If you shout, your children will shout too. In fact, your children will use *your* language, so if you bitch about other people, they will become bitchy too. If you tell them your own fears – about global warming, for example, or about how a particular election result will prove to be a disaster for the country – they may become even more worried than you are, and may even fear that the world is about to come to an end. If you have a fear of spiders, 'sort your fear out', because no matter how hard you try to cover it up, your kids will sense it and they may develop a similar fear themselves.

Try to diffuse situations by being positive and avoiding drama. For example, if your child doesn't get a part in the school play or get picked for the football team, don't buy into the drama. Instead, say, 'It will be fine. Something better will happen. It will work out AMAZINGLY well.' Or 'Maybe you will get in next time.'

Your words are powerful, so be careful about the words you use

If you call your child a pest, they may grow up to think that they are getting in the way of other people. If you call your child naughty, they will live up to their reputation. Instead of branding them with names, try to distract them from negative behaviour.

Stay positive and calm and say, 'It will all work out AMAZINGLY well.'

Be a great role model

If you are having an emotional meltdown in your life, don't expect your kids to be your carers. Instead, sort yourself out by getting outside help. Protect your children from hearing your negative story. If what you want to say is not going to enhance their lives, don't say it at all.

If you cry when your children go to university, go away on holiday without you or leave home, you need to find hobbies or work to fill the void. Use the techniques in this book to help you build the next AMAZING phase of your life. Your children should be able to get on with their own lives without having to worry about you. And you should be delighted for your children when they are getting on with the adventure of their lives.

If you make demands on your children and ask them to sort out your problems, be aware of what you are doing, sort out your own problems and set them free. Your children are not there to be your counsellor, to sort out your money, marriage, work or health problems.

Perhaps your own parents have put you in the role of problem solver for them. If so, start to set boundaries by telling them, 'You will be able to sort this out.' Believe that there are AMAZING ways to sort things out, as everything can improve and be resolved. Don't be at the beck and call of your children or your parents. If you, your adult children and your parents all lived on different continents, you would all have to sort out your own problems. Obviously, there may come a time when your parents are old and need support. But wait until these issues arise and then find the most AMAZING ways to deal with them.

- Get the balance right between support and independence for you, your children and your parents.

- Teach your sons and daughters to be decent people who respect all other people, animals and the environment.

- Explain things to your children in a way that is appropriate for their age. Sometimes, they need to know things, whereas at other times it may be better to protect them from negative news that they don't really need to know about.

Teach and guide

You can teach children something or nothing using the same activity. Imagine two separate, unrelated parents in two different gardens in the autumn time. The first parent says to his children, 'Mind the tree roots. Don't trip over. Don't get your hands dirty. Be careful of the prickly holly.' The other parent asks his children to help collect the autumn leaves and put them in a sack. The sack fills up quickly and when the children think it's full, the parent tells them to stand on top of it to compress the leaves and make room for more. The children in the second garden are enjoying themselves more than the ones being micro-managed by the obsessive parent. The parent in the first garden is teaching his children nothing other than fear and that the garden holds all sorts of dangers, while the parent in the second garden is teaching his children lessons and skills.

Let your children make their own choices and decisions from an early age. Let them take part in choosing presents for friends and family. And let them choose what to wear as soon as they want to do this. You don't need to give them a full choice from every item of clothing they possess. Just give them a limited choice between a couple of outfits. As they get older and can make decisions more quickly, you can give them more choice. Your clothes say a lot about you, so let your children's personalities flourish. By allowing them to develop confidence about who they are, they will learn to be independent too. If you are in the habit of taking control of their choices, they will grow up questioning their own decisions.

Coffee and doughnuts

Take time to connect with your children. A trip to a café just to sit and hear what they have to say is a good way to catch up with each other without the distractions of home. (Turn your phone off!) Try to have individual time with each of your children. Don't make excuses that there is no time. Make it possible: 'I can do it. I am doing. It is done. I make it a priority.'

Rearrange your life to schedule communication time with your children. Have a relaxed time together and be interested in them and their lives. Talk about your life too, so that they get used to discussions not just being about them. A good communicator will ask questions and be interested in other people. So teach them this. Talk about subjects that interest them. Build a relationship that will last a lifetime. Love them and accept them. If they don't live up to your expectations, just accept that. If you don't get along with your kids today, will you ever? Many people don't talk to their parents or siblings. Will you be the kind of parent that is visited out of a sense of duty rather than because your children really want to spend time with you? It all begins now.

Communicating

I often watch parents in cafés. Some of them micro-manage their children, some ignore them and immerse themselves in a computer or phone, and some have enjoyable conversations with them.

Communicate with your children face to face. Sit at the table as a family to eat your evening meals. If you have nothing to say to your children, ask yourself why? What could I do better? Read your children's body language. If they shrink back when you say something, talk about something more positive that interests them.

If you are a single parent or divorced, don't talk about your ex-partner or your love life in front of your children. Think before you speak.

Distract

One day, I saw a small child having a tantrum in a London Underground station. The mother was telling him to stop and to stand still, but he carried on. There were some aeroplane posters on the wall in front of them and the mother could have distracted the child by saying, 'Wow, look at the aeroplanes!' But she was so wrapped up in his behaviour she didn't even notice them.

Look for things around you to distract your child from bad behaviour. If you are frustrated, your child probably will be too. The mum at the Underground station may have been tired, but sometimes it is less tiring to have a distraction conversation rather than a battle. Always plan ahead and have an activity bag with you, as small children get bored easily when travelling or in restaurants.

Your children learn from the conversations they have with you. Don't rely on technology to entertain them or sit them down in front of the TV and ignore them. Limit their daily TV viewing and make time to talk to them. When your children are small, inspire them with subjects they are interested in by doing things like going to museums, looking at nature or books.

- The little girl who played an art auction board game and was taken to art galleries by her grandparents went on to study History of Art at university and to do a masters degree in Art Business in Paris. She then ended up working in an auction house.

Remember that whatever your children are surrounded by can become part of them.

Protect your children

You decide what to surround your children with and your reaction to life will influence them. If you choose to have magazines on the coffee table full of negative images of people and you don't explain to your children that the behaviour depicted isn't normal behaviour, they will grow up thinking it's fine. If you let them watch horror films or play violent games, their impressionable minds will be influenced by violence and horror, which may cause them to be scared, worried, have nightmares or be violent themselves. Think very carefully about what you are letting your children view.

The last thing a child hears before they fall asleep will remain in their mind throughout the night. So I suggest that you only allow your children to hear positive, calming music at bedtime or positive recordings before they go to sleep.

I have had many child clients who were used to watching violent films or negative news items before they went to bed and who then had nightmares triggered by this material.

- Make sure your children are exposed only to age-appropriate material.

- Take away their phones at bedtime.

- Control what games they play, even if it means not allowing them to play the ones their friends play.

- Put parental controls on your computer to protect your children.

- Limit their access to social media.

- Help your children develop healthy interests, such as cooking, sport, art, making things, dance.

- Explain that there are lots of good things going on in the world, not just the negative things shown on the news.

- Let your children sort out their own issues. Give them advice, but let them stand up for themselves.

- Protect your child from an abusive sibling. Don't assume that you can't do anything and that it is normal behaviour – it is not.

- If your young child doesn't like going to the crèche, find a way to make it work. Don't blame them because they won't do what the other kids do. Tell yourself, 'It's all working out AMAZINGLY well.'

- If your child is at boarding school and doesn't like being there, listen to them and do what you can to change the situation.

- Teach your children that everyone is doing their best with the knowledge they have, even if their best is not great.

- Teach your children to be around people who are good for them.

Being a good parent

Anyone from any background can be a good or a bad parent. The one thing all parents have in common is that they can improve their parenting. Make a conscious effort to improve your relationship with your children, starting right now. Get the balance right between being involved and knowing when to say nothing. Teach your children to be kind to other people. Teach them to be thoughtful, maybe by making a birthday card or present for someone. If they forget to buy you a birthday card someday, don't let it upset you. Just remind them gently for next time and accept the fact that they may have other things on their mind.

Make life fun

Learning something in a fun way from an early age creates a happy memory for children.

- If you play waiters and waitresses to clear the dishes from the table, they will always be willing to help in the kitchen because it will be associated with a happy feeling.

- If you play a hairdresser or barber game when you wash their hair, they will actually look forwards to their hair being washed.

- If you play nice music and have a sing-along while you tidy up together, they will always enjoy putting things away.

- If they tidy their room while being timed against the clock as a game, they will be happy to pick up their clothes and tidy up after themselves.

If your sons and daughters know how to look after themselves and are respectful and helpful, they will grow up to have happy relationships or marriages.

Working parents and stay-at-home parents

Some people feel guilty if they work and have to leave their young children in childcare or leave older teenagers at home on their own. Others feel bad if they stay at home and don't have a career or earn money. And many people feel that they are being judged by other parents or family members for the decisions they make about parenting.

Everyone is different before they have children – some have careers while others don't. So they will be different after they have had children too. It is up to you as parents to find out what works best for you and your family, as there is not one way of doing things. It doesn't really matter how you organize things and whether you work or stay at home, as long as it works for you.

Be supportive of other parents whether they work or stay at home. Remember that other people are individuals too and it is none of your business how they decide to do things. Many of my female clients tell me that they feel confused about what is right for them after they have had children. I always encourage them to steer their lives and careers in the best direction for them. You need to follow your heart. You need to get the balance right.

Don't allow your children to be an excuse to stop you building a secure financial future and career. Instead, say, 'I have AMAZING work which is highly paid and fits in with the children. I have AMAZING childcare solutions.' If you think AMAZING, you will find AMAZING solutions and the right balance. I have seen this time and time again with clients. For example, there will be other mothers who are happy to earn some extra money childminding, while your kids will be happy to have the chance to go to a friend's house and will gain independence from being in the company of others.

If you are self-employed, it can be useful to pay for more childcare to give you more focused time to get more work done. You will find that your earnings will increase overall when you pay for extra childcare. It's probably best to pay for your children to be looked after for a whole day rather than an hour or two here and there, so that you have a full working day and time to get into the rhythm of working.

Flowing with work

You may have to tailor your career at different stages of your life. So just flow with what works at each stage as the children's needs change. Imagine the lives of you and your children running smoothly in parallel with each other, like railway tracks.

Teach your children about money

Your children need to learn about managing their money so that they develop the skills that will enable them to manage their finances in the real world. Encourage them to save their pocket money and birthday money. Teach them to budget. It is all about choices and decisions. If they choose to spend their money on one thing, it won't be there if they want to purchase something else in the future. Teach them to save most of what they receive by always putting a portion of it into a savings account.

I gave a copy of my hypnotherapy recording *Money – Increase your Wealth* to my window cleaner, who was complaining that his grown-up son's spending was out of control and that he had to keep bailing him out financially.

I realized that he had some financial boundary issues with his son, which my recording would resolve. When he came back to clean my windows six weeks later, he had put his prices up. I was really proud of him for being able to ask for more money. It did make me laugh, though, the fact that he charged me more when I was the person who had given him the 'increase your wealth' recording! The hypnotherapy had given him the confidence to charge more and feel good about it. As a result, he ended up being £500 per month better off, which is quite a significant increase – and he decided to let his son take responsibility for his own finances.

In-laws

Your in-laws can be useful to you, so be grateful for any help you get from them. If they are willing to look after your children to give you a break, let them. Accept that they may have ways of doing things that are different from the way you do them. If your relationship with your in-laws is strained, try to see the situations as cartoons so that you can laugh at them rather than feeling angry.

Remember that your in-laws have been affected throughout their lives by all the issues in this book. However they behave, they are doing the best they can, just like everyone else. If you have in-laws you can't get along with and who seem to be intent on destroying your marriage if you allow them to, imagine 'AMAZING solutions' and 'everything working out well'. If your partner isn't able to stand up to his or her parents, accept this and find a way to navigate around them.

Children and separation/divorce

If you are in a bad relationship, you need to do everything possible to sort things out. I believe the techniques in this book will help you to resolve most relationship issues. If you do decide to go your separate ways, you have a responsibility to support your children financially as well as emotionally and to make every effort to see them regularly. Learn from past mistakes and make sure that you don't end up in another destructive relationship.

If you are divorced, keep in contact with your children, even if they don't seem to be interested in you. Everyone needs to feel they are wanted. Your children may be under pressure from people around them to say that they don't want to see you. Rise above any mess you and your ex-partner have created by being the adult and doing everything you can to keep your relationships going with your children.

Make regular contact by sending them letters or parcels. Send them pocket money every week so that they feel they have regular contact with you. If you are not sure whether your ex-partner is allowing your children to receive the post you send them, photocopy your letters so that one day, when your children are grown-up, you can show them that you did try to make contact.

If you do get regular contact with your children, don't just turn on the TV and expect them to entertain themselves. Make the time you spend together really special so that they have happy memories of being with you and want to see you more often.

- Find your special niche role within your children's lives.

- Do not say negative things to your children about your ex-partner. Try to say AMAZING things about their other parent and something AMAZING about yourself, too.

When is the right time to have children?

If you have children when you are younger, you may be less financially secure, your career may just be starting, you may miss out on going out and having fun with friends and you may struggle with the responsibility. But you will benefit later, as you will have time to get on with your life once your children have grown up.

If you have children later, you will probably be more financially stable and more mature, and therefore more able to cope. But you may struggle to adjust, perhaps because you are set in your own ways and possibly less physically fit.

Whatever age you are when you have your children, sacrifices will have to be made, as they are by any parent. If you think you had your kids at the wrong time, just accept the way things have happened and don't wallow in self-pity. If you had been meant to have them at a different time, you would have done so. Be open to taking advice from experienced parents who have already been there and done it.

The realities of having children are not really spoken about to young women, so there is no information stored in their subconscious mind about how to cope while working or taking a career break to have kids. Consequently, I see increasing numbers of women who struggle to accept parenting. The subconscious mind holds our beliefs, which are programmed into it over a lifetime.

So, if the plan of being a mum is not in your subconscious mind because you have been programmed to want to have a career, it can feel unnatural to give up part of your life to have children. I think that understanding and accepting these feelings can help you to come to terms with them. It is okay to feel the way you do. Women all over the world come to terms with similar feelings every day. And it isn't just a problem that is faced by women. If young men haven't formed habits in the subconscious mind of being a responsible parent and fitting their lives around their children, they may struggle with parenting later too.

The techniques in this book will help you to adjust to the changes. Try to flow with parenting. Instead of feeling trapped, imagine a wiggly string leading you on an adventure.

Wishing you hadn't had children

Some women feel complete when they have children. Some wish they had not had them at all. And some feel regret as a passing thought from time to time. Parenting can be a real challenge for some people. But I suggest that you surrender to it rather than battling against it. Just hold your hands up, surrender, accept that this is where you are and feel relief that you haven't got to fight it any more.

It is okay to feel the way you do. You are an individual. You always were and you always will be. Say to yourself, 'AMAZING things come from being a parent.' Get into the flow of parenting and allow your children to enable you to experience and understand a whole other side to life. Let it be an adventure.

Manage your feelings by making sure you get some quality time for yourself every week. And arrange time with your partner so that the kids don't take over completely. If you are a single parent, you need to have quality time with friends. By being creative, you will find ways to get the balance right. Always believing that things will work out AMAZINGLY well will allow good things to happen. In your mind, notice the good things about having children. If you feel that having children has stretched you financially, remember that it is just a phase that will last until they grow up. You may not be able to do or afford the things you used to do and afford, but one day they will be possible again.

You may feel at times, 'I can't deal with the kids. They drive me insane. I can't cope.' If that happens, remind yourself that this stage is not going to last forever.

Parenting is a series of phases that culminate in the children growing up and taking responsibility for themselves. In the meantime, do things differently. Make better choices and decisions and find easier ways to deal with them. Identify what is actually causing you stress – it might be their homework or the whole bedtime routine – and then sort it out.

Say, 'I can do this. I am doing it. It is done.' SMILE and laugh at this stage as if it is a funny, crazy TV sitcom!

There is always a solution to every problem that occurs with children. Change something to get a different result. For instance, have bath time before the evening meal or get your child to phone a school friend for help with their homework – after all, their friend was in the lesson and you weren't.

Build a life for yourself too

Remember, your life and the lives of your children should run in parallel with each other. There will be times when they are younger when you have to do more for them. But build a life for yourself along the way. Having your own life will also help you to avoid empty nest syndrome when your children leave home.

Some women love mothering, so when their kids leave home they feel as though they have lost a job they will never get back. You could slip into depression because of that loss if you are not careful.

A friend told me that she had cried every day for two months when her daughter went to university. 'Well, nothing has changed,' I told her. 'You cried every day for weeks when your daughter went to nursery.' I also reminded my friend that she was removed from the school hall by the headmistress during a parent induction meeting when her daughter started infant school because her crying was upsetting the other parents! 'It's about time for you to break the habit of crying over your children,' I said. And she agreed that her behaviour was ridiculous.

I would suggest that if you are upset because your parenting has come to an end, you should fill your time helping some of the many children who need support and guidance, either in a voluntary or a paid role. Let your children see you getting on with your life so that they can happily get on with theirs.

- Don't be the extreme parent.

- Be happy to see your children moving on to the next stage of their lives.

- Celebrate their progress.

- Don't let parenting be an excuse not to build a great life for yourself.

Kite technique

Imagine you and your children are in a beautiful place, perhaps on a beach or on a grassy hillside. Allow your imagination to take you to somewhere that feels special for you. Imagine each of you has a kite that you are flying. Imagine that you are all in control of your own kites. Imagine that each of you navigates your kite around everyone else's. Each kite is doing well. They are all close to each other, but they are free to move in the sky around each other. Some kites fly high, while others are at a lower height. You are all smiling as you fly the kites. The kites remind you that you can all work well together and individually, too. Repeat this exercise, which will remind you of each person's individuality.

Enjoy your children

If you are relaxed, happy, balanced and positive at each stage of your children's lives, they will be those things too, and you will have good friendships with them for life. Remember that your children need to be free. If they choose to live on the other side of the world, you must let them go. Make sure you have a full and interesting life at every stage, alongside your children.

Be a balanced version of yourself around your children. See the good in them and teach them to be good versions of themselves, too. SMILE and allow your relationships with your children to flourish into something quite AMAZING.

You are your children's future. Invest in good parenting to make their future bright.

Cut the crap from parenting and feel AMAZING.

Chapter summary

✂ Be interested in your children, but also let them be independent.

✂ Explain why we do things.

✂ Be reasonable.

✂ Don't rescue your children every time they fall down. If you do, they will always expect to be picked up.

✂ Use the techniques in this book to help you to be a calm, rational parent.

✂ 'Snapshot' happy moments in your mind when you are enjoying your children to build your AMAZING zone bank.

✂ Use the red triangle technique: visualize a red triangle and put your worries into it. Then shrink it down as you let go and the stresses dissolve.

✂ Visualize your children grown up and having positive relationships with them.

✂ Let being a parent be a positive adventure.

✂ Say, 'It's all working out AMAZINGLY well.'

✂ Use the wiggly string technique: visualize a wiggly string leading you to everything you need in order to have a smooth parenting experience.

✂ Use the kite technique: visualize you and your children flying kites. See them as capable and in charge of their own kites. See you all working well as a team, navigating around each other's kites, and feel relaxed.

STEP 1. Surrender to parenting.

STEP 2. Everything is just a phase. Enjoy each phase.

STEP 3. Build a relationship that will last a lifetime.

Believe in AMAZING possibilities. Piece your life together like a jigsaw puzzle and make it a wonderful experience.

CHAPTER 17

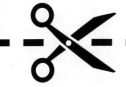

CUT THE EXCUSES AND FEEL AT HOME IN YOUR LIFE

People often won't venture out of their comfort zone. Instead, they make up all sorts of excuses to avoid change. Listen to yourself so that you can be aware of when you are making an excuse. Make a very conscious effort to change.

Work on yourself. Don't rescue others. Rescue yourself first. Put your energy into creating the life you want. Other people will find their way in their own time when they are ready.

While it is nice to help other people, it is also important not to waste time on people who use excuses to avoid changing. Be aware when people are putting barriers in their way so that they are unable to progress their lives. Consciously pull back and let them get on with their own lives. Avoid spending time listening to people who say the same negative things over and over again but who don't action change. Try to learn from their behaviour so that you are aware of sometimes behaving in the same way in some areas of your life.

Remember that some people may not be as ready for change as you are. Using the information in this book, I believe anyone can change for the better. Make a point of identifying excuses and eliminate them from your life.

- Let go of weight-loss excuses.

- Let go of drinking excuses.

- Let go of career excuses.

- Let go of money excuses.

- Let go of family problem excuses.

- Let go of exercise excuses.

Let excuses pass like clouds in the sky. Wave goodbye to them, rub, tap or press your left knuckles as you say, 'Let it pass. Let it go.'

Replace excuses with AMAZING choices and decisions.

Excuses are the main reason for people not creating an AMAZING life

I have helped hundreds of people reduce their alcohol intake using hypnotherapy. A common excuse I have often heard over the years is that they don't have 15 minutes per day to listen to my recordings. I explain that they are wasting hours of their life every evening by sitting on the couch drunk. By listening to a recording for 15 minutes a day, they will become sober and have whole evenings to do what they want. Spending 15 minutes now will give them back a lot more time in the future. There is always another way of seeing things. I have never had a client who hasn't been happy to have reduced the amount of alcohol they were drinking. Sometimes change can be scary, but try to see it as an adventure and know it will work out AMAZINGLY well.

Find a way to make things happen

Some people make one excuse after another without even knowing they are making them, because it has become normal for them to avoid change. It is sometimes difficult to identify where the excuses are. But every time you are not at least open to a suggestion from someone else, an excuse is sure to be creeping in. Although you don't need to do whatever has been suggested, you may learn from someone else's ideas. It's easy to be quite defensive, bearing in mind past judgement by parents, teachers and friends, and most adults have a built-in defence mechanism, which stops them from being open to change. Make a point yourself of always being open to change.

The fact that you are reading this book probably means that you *are* ready to make changes in your life. Read the book, reread it, dip in and out of it and make it an AMAZING way of life. Begin by changing everyday routines – move the kettle, move the food around in the kitchen cupboards, take a new route to work, walk a different way around the supermarket, or even do your shopping in a different shop. Create as many small changes as you can so that you feel your life flowing in a new direction. Self-talk yourself into the positive: 'I can do it. I am doing it. It is done.'

- Change will set you free.

Autumn leaves technique

Imagine brightly coloured autumn leaves blowing in the breeze on a large oak tree. Imagine the leaves falling one by one from the tree branches. Imagine the breeze blowing them high up into the air so that they dance through the sky. Imagine the leaves being swept along into the distance until they gradually disappear. You can take as much time as you like to do this as you let go of each leaf. As you imagine the leaves blowing in the breeze, allow all the excuses to release from your mind. Feel the feeling of a cooling breeze sweeping around the trees, moving the leaves gently from the branches as you easily allow the excuses to disappear into the distance along with the leaves.

When you are ready, imagine the tree ready for new buds to grow and flourish, just as your ideas are able to flourish, too, as you feel ready for a fresh start to make good things happen for you. Gradually imagine the new green leaves, bright and fresh, with the sunlight dancing across them as they gently blow in the spring air. Imagine your ideas flourishing as you develop your positive ideas and life. Make positive choices and decisions as you allow life to flourish.

Repeat this exercise occasionally to help move your mind forwards to new and better things.

Be enthusiastic, train yourself to think of things you can do and start believing in yourself

You don't need to know what is around the next corner. Just do what feels right to get to the corner so that you have a chance to see around it. You don't need to know your whole life plan. Just do something to get yourself moving forwards. Don't be the person who lets life pass them by. Instead, encourage yourself. See a wiggly string leading you to everything you need to find along the way.

- Cut the excuses from your life and feel AMAZING.

Your life is like a home

You can choose what you do and don't want to have in your life. Think of your life as being similar to your home. You can choose how to decorate and furnish where you live. You may de-clutter from time to time, getting rid of old things you don't want any more. Well, your life is the same. There may be things you have outgrown and other things you aspire to have. It is a good idea regularly to take a look at where you are in your life so that you can identify what you can 'bring in' or 'take out' to improve it. And it is also a good idea to de-clutter your real home, as it is a reflection of who you are.

Surround yourself with things that remind you of the life you aspire to have, such as books about successful people, fresh flowers, car magazines, positive pictures on the walls, perhaps including a picture of your degree certificate or photographs of happy holidays, and cushions with words written on them such as 'happy', 'calm', 'love' 'AMAZING' – in fact, anything that works for you. Surrounding yourself with a taste of the lifestyle you want will help you to create that life. You may not own that Manhattan penthouse apartment yet, but a book on your coffee table about New York skylines will make you SMILE every time you see it and will help you to feel closer to that dream. Be selective about 'what' and 'who' you put into your life and into your home. Feel at home in your life and in your home.

Heart cupboard technique

Imagine a cupboard or cabinet in your mind. Imagine it is heart-shaped or has a heart design on it. Visualize opening the doors to reveal the contents. Imagine taking the contents out. Let go of the clutter, throw things away, have a good clear-out. As you do this, imagine your mind and your body can let go of past emotions. As you sort through the contents of the cupboard, let your mind let go of the negative past, put the now and the future in place. Make a conscious decision to put back only what is useful to you and the things that inspire you. Feel your heart filled with warmth and happiness as you SMILE and say 'It's AMAZING'.

Much of your life is good, so make sure to keep hold of the things you have now which are useful and keep some positive things from the past. But make the cupboard comfortable so that your heart is filled with joy. You can decide what you would like to put in the cupboard. Let the clutter dissolve and let your heart cupboard fill up with happy, warm-hearted, homely feelings, allowing the changes to happen at a pace that feels right for you.

Repeat this exercise, maybe each time with different things in the cupboard.

Your surroundings will filter into your subconscious mind, programming you to create the life they represent and making you believe that it is possible to live the life you want to live.

Cut the clutter from your life and feel AMAZING.

Chapter summary

✂ Spend time with people who are good for you.

✂ Have quality time with your family.

✂ Have quality time with yourself.

✂ Have quality rest and relaxation.

✂ Enjoy the skills you have at work.

✂ Build upon your skills.

✂ Be clever with your money.

✂ Be kind and treat other people well.

✂ Respect yourself and your body.

✂ Respect women, men, children, animals and the environment you are in.

✂ Support charities you believe in.

✂ Use the autumn leaves technique: let the leaves blow into the distance as excuses dissolve. Allow the new spring buds to grow. Allow your ideas to flourish.

✂ Use the heart-shaped cupboard technique: de-clutter the heart cupboard to allow the warm-hearted, homely feelings to flourish in your life.

STEP 1. Live the best life you can.

STEP 2. Make your life AMAZING.

STEP 3. Live a life that makes you SMILE.

ABOUT THE AUTHOR

Stephen Payne

Ailsa Frank is a self-help author, motivational coach and leading hypnotherapist with a compassionate yet no-nonsense approach. She is well known for helping people with heartbreak, alcohol, money, relationship, health, confidence and emotional issues. Through workshops, one-to-one therapy and her range of hypnosis downloads, Ailsa has already helped thousands of people improve their lives.

Ailsa was a successful career woman until, in 2002, her life fell apart following divorce, mental breakdown and losing custody of her daughter. She chose not to take anti-depressants, and instead decided to face her problems head-on by changing her mindset and her life. Having worked out how to help herself, she initially set a goal to help one other person, as she believes that 'every life matters'.

In 2005 Ailsa retrained and qualified as a hypnotherapist. She now draws on her own life experiences to help others overcome the difficulties they face and to become the best they can be. She wrote *Cut the Crap and Feel Amazing* to share with people the answers and tools they need to cope with the stress of everyday living, and the events happening in the world.

Ailsa loves a simple life with cute dogs, spas, happiness and afternoon tea.

 @AilsaFrank    AilsaFrank

 ailsafrank   Ailsa Frank Author and Hypnotherapist

www.ailsafrank.com

HAY HOUSE
Look within

Join the conversation about latest products, events, exclusive offers and more.

f Hay House UK

🐦 @HayHouseUK

📷 @hayhouseuk

♥ healyourlife.com

We'd love to hear from you!

Printed in the United States
by Baker & Taylor Publisher Services